MOON
GARDEN

MOON GARDEN

A GUIDE TO CREATING AN EVENING OASIS

Jarema Osofsky

Photographs by Kate S. Jordan
Illustrations by Jill DeHaan

CHRONICLE BOOKS
SAN FRANCISCO

Library of Congress Cataloging-in-Publication Data
Names: Osofsky, Jarema, author. | Jordan, Kate S.,
    photographer. | De Haan,Jill, illustrator.
Title: Moon garden : a guide to creating an evening
    oasis / Jarema Osofsky; photographs by Kate S. Jordan ;
    illustrations by Jill De Haan.
Description: San Francisco : Chronicle Books, [2023] |
    Summary: "A guide to designing and planting a moon
    garden"-- Provided by publisher.
Identifiers: LCCN 2023008764 | ISBN 9781797219936
    (hardcover)
Subjects: LCSH: Night gardens. | Night-flowering plants. |
    Night-fragrant flowers. | Handbooks and manuals.
Classification: LCC SB433.6 .O76 2023 | DDC 635.9/53-
    -dc23/eng/20230501 LC record available at https://lccn.
    loc.gov/2023008764

Manufactured in China.

Photographs by Kate S. Jordan.
Photo assisting by Sam Kang.
Illustrations by Jill DeHaan.
Design by Lizzie Vaughan.
Typeset in Coolumbus, Gilroy, and SangBleu.

10 9 8 7 6 5 4 3 2 1

Chronicle books and gifts are available at special quantity
discounts to corporations, professional associations,
literacy programs, and other organizations. For details
and discount information, please contact our premiums
department at corporatesales@chroniclebooks.com or at
1-800-759-0190.

Chronicle Books LLC
680 Second Street
San Francisco, California 94107
www.chroniclebooks.com

FOR MY SISTER, LULING, AND TOPANGA

CONTENTS

INTRODUCTION
What Is a Moon Garden?

A couple of summers ago, as the evening sky faded to indigo, I settled into some dunes at the beach with a small group of friends. We'd come to watch the moon rise. To the sound of lapping waves, and as stars began to populate the sky, we drank ginger tea and waited. First, a sliver peeped above the horizon, then a heavy, amber orb slowly rose to bathe the night sky in its glowing light. A wave of calm and wonder washed over me as I marveled at this spectacle. Afterward, while walking back to my friend's house, I paused to observe the neighbors' gardens. Under the cover of night, I could smell thickets of night-blooming jasmine; I saw bougainvillea weeping over fences and climbing moonflowers reflecting the moon's soft glow. The world looked totally different at night, and it was surprising how much shone in the darkness.

Each night, as twilight turns to darkness, a secret world awakens. Diurnal plants like tulips and poppies close their petals for slumber, while nocturnal plants like evening primrose and nicotiana bask in the moonlight, releasing their sweet and spicy scents and drawing in nocturnal pollinators like moths and bats to delight in their pollen. While any garden can be beautiful at night, some gardens are planted specifically with evening in mind. These are called moon gardens. Filled with lush night-blooming and night-fragrant plants, with white flowers and silver foliage that reflect the soft light, the moon garden is an evocative and serene oasis to relax in after a day of work.

Whether during the day or night, spending time outside and with plants is hugely beneficial for mental and physical health. Studies have shown that walking barefoot on the earth for fifteen minutes a day can significantly reduce stress, anxiety, and inflammation. Recall a time you walked barefoot on the earth, sat quietly among the trees, or picked berries off the vine and felt relaxed or rejuvenated. It's restorative to reconnect with the land. In Japan, it is common to practice "forest bathing," or *shinrin-yoku*, which means letting nature into the body through the five senses: seeing, hearing, touching, smelling, and tasting.

Yet in today's work culture it can be difficult to make time to get outdoors and immerse yourself in nature. Carving out time in the garden can feel like an unobtainable luxury. But once the workday and errands are done, the evening invites you to enjoy your garden "after hours," in the moonlight.

In the early days of running my garden design business, Dirt Queen NYC, I had to be out in the field meeting clients, sourcing plants at nurseries, managing installs, and planting gardens; more often than not, my hands were happily in the soil and my nails full of dirt. I also operated a by-appointment plant shop in my studio, open only on the weekends, which became known as Brooklyn's "plant speakeasy." Most evenings I spent on my computer catching up on emails and finishing designs late into the night. I did not create space to truly decompress from work because I was building a business and there was always something more to do. After several years of this, my mind and body were exhausted. Ironically, my quest to create sustainable gardens for my clients made my own lifestyle unsustainable. So I made a commitment to listen to my body's natural rhythms, respect my circadian clock, and rest in the evenings. I made a conscious effort to turn off screens and do things I enjoyed, which brought me outdoors. I journaled in the garden, dined with friends, and took nightly walks with my partner Adam and corgi Topanga, searching for the moon and admiring flowers. Inhaling their scent became a nightly ritual for me, and as the rest of the world slept, I felt alive and connected to the plant life all around me. Remembering that night on the beach when I watched the moon rise, I was inspired to recreate that lustrous experience in my own garden.

The impact of any garden space can be profound, and a moon garden is a special invitation. The darkness, subtly illuminated by the moon, heightens our senses. Without the distractions of a full field of color, our eyes can better notice the shimmer of petals and the arresting fragrance of blossoms. And you don't need a lot of space to experience these effects. You can create a moon garden on a small terrace or rooftop, in a backyard, or even indoors if you don't have outdoor space. Gardens of any size are restorative—places for growth, life, and healing. Your garden can be a sanctuary under the stars, and the moon can be a gentle, steadfast guide. Working with the moon's energy, even metaphorically, allows you to cultivate a spiritual practice that nurtures you while you nurture your garden. Your moon garden can be not only the site of spiritual practices such as meditation, journaling, and healing rituals, but also the practice itself, in planting and tending to its growth.

This book is both an ode to
the beauty of moon gardens
and a guide for creating and
caring for your own moon
garden. We will dive into
the world of night-blooming
plants, night-fragrant plants,
and region-specific plants.
You'll find design guidance,
horticultural advice, and tips
for making the garden a sanctuary for your own enjoyment.
This book will also immerse
you in ideas of biophilia—the
notion that humans possess
an innate tendency to seek
connections with nature and
other forms of life—inviting
you, through meditative
prompts and rituals, to make
such connections. In the process, you'll dig your fingers
into the earth. Ultimately,
I hope that by the time you
finish this book, you will have
your very own moon garden,
a site for holistic, contempla-
tive practices that nurtures
your inner self.

MOON GARDENS THROUGHOUT HISTORY

The desire to create and enjoy a moonlit garden goes back centuries. From medieval Japanese rock gardens to the Mehtab Bagh garden built by a Mughal emperor in the sixteenth century, people have long devoted energy and resources to serene landscapes that shimmer in the night.

In addition to designing moon gardens dedicated to evening enjoyment, various communities through the ages have also farmed and planted gardens based on the lunar phases. It's clear that the moon has played a central role in gardening, and it still does to this day.

A Brief History

In fifteenth-century Japan, the aesthetically minded shogun Ashikaga Yoshimasa had the Ginkaku-ji, or Silver Pavilion, built as his retirement villa and gardens in Kyoto. He commissioned the artist Sōami, considered the greatest garden designer in medieval Japan, to design the gardens. The garden features a magnificent cone-shaped structure sculpted from white sand, named Kogetsudai ("moon-viewing platform"). It is surrounded by the Ginshadan, an expanse of sand finely raked in concentric circles radiating outward, emulating water ripples in a pond. Japanese myths state that the Kogetsudai was built to sit upon and watch the moon rise above the eastern mountains, and the expanse of white sand was intended to reflect the moonlight.

Situated directly across from the Taj Mahal, the Mehtab Bagh garden, or Moonlight Garden, was built in the sixteenth century by Emperor Babur as a pleasure garden in the Islamic style. It was a place primarily to view—and pay homage to— the Taj Mahal. Replete with lavish pavilions, marble fountains, white pathways, and reflecting pools, the garden was designed for the enjoyment of Mughal nobility, especially in the evenings after the day's heat had subsided. Night-blooming red cedar (*Toona ciliata*) and white-blossomed champaca trees (*Magnolia champaca*) both filled the air with fragrance. The lotus pool was another stunning central feature. A dramatic raised octagonal terrace offered a view of both the moonlit Taj Mahal and its reflection in the shimmering water.

One of the earliest recorded moon gardens in the United States belonged to Benjamin Poore, a newspaper correspondent and author who, in the 1830s, designed a garden unlike any other at his home in Indian Hill, Massachusetts. Expansive floral beds featuring white flowers of all varieties, radiant in the moonlight, spanned 700 feet (213 meters) along a hillside path. Star of Bethlehem, daffodils, candytuft, and arches of honeysuckle, among many other garden species, entranced the night visitor. A bit of a color absolutist, Poore extended his love of white beyond flora and into fauna: Herds of white cattle roamed his land along with flocks of sheep, white oxen, white pigeons, doves, chickens, and a resident white dog. (Rumor had it that he even kept white peacocks, but that's never been confirmed.)

If ever there was a moon garden to rival all others, it would be the garden designed by legendary writer Vita Sackville-West in Kent, England, in the 1930s. At Sissinghurst Castle she created what is now known simply as the White Garden on the surrounding grounds (see page 18)—which were in a state of ruin when she bought the estate. With her husband, Harold Nicolson, and a team of gardeners, Sackville-West spent thirty years reviving the land and cultivating a glamorous garden.

In a signature style blending wit, charm, and lyricism, she wrote about her gardening adventures and misadventures in her weekly *Observer* column, "In Your Garden." She observed,

> My grey, green, and white garden will have the advantage of a high yew hedge behind it, a wall along one side, a strip of box edging along another side.... There will be white pansies, and white peonies, and white irises with their grey leaves . . . at least, I hope there will be all these things. I don't want to boast in advance . . . it may be a terrible failure.

The garden was in fact terribly successful. Still celebrated as one of the world's most beautiful, it's visited annually by thousands of plant enthusiasts.

The moon garden at Sissinghurst was one of many "garden rooms" Sackville-West designed. She was one of the first gardeners to employ this concept of garden rooms—enclosed garden spaces fed into by axial walkways. The moon garden room featured walls of pale stones and an enchanting floral collection of white delphinium, foxglove, hydrangea, silver mounds of artemisia, and regal lilies (to name a few) in a palette limited to white, grays, and greens. Sackville-West relished the challenges of color play within this restricted palette: "[Color play] is something more than merely interesting. It is great fun and endlessly amusing as an experiment, capable of perennial improvement, as you take away the things that don't fit in . . . and replace them by something you like better."

Gardening with the Lunar Phases

For millennia, the moon has been a powerful guide for farming and agriculture. Farming communities dating back to the Babylonian era believed that celestial bodies dictated the seasons and influenced the lives of plants and animals. Agricultural calendars were determined by the position of the stars in the night sky, planetary orbits, and the celestial gods that ruled these planets. Rituals and feasts won the favor of these gods. Seeds were planted according to lunar calendars that were based on recorded observations and wisdom passed down through generations. Such practices are still followed in many places today.

BIODYNAMIC GARDENING

Gardening with the phases of the moon has come to be known by another name: biodynamic gardening. It's a method of gardening (and, notably, farming) in alignment with lunar phases and other planetary cycles. Its holistic approach rests on a few important principles, including an understanding of cosmology, an ecological mindfulness of all living things, and compassionate, ethical stewardship of the land.

Through a series of agricultural lectures delivered in 1924, Austrian philosopher Rudolf Steiner founded the biodynamic movement, spearheading the first of many future organic farming movements. Steiner sought to integrate farming practices from ancient folk traditions with contemporary scientific methods, and his teachings stressed the interconnectedness and interdependence of all living things. He saw the farm as a world unto itself that could and should be self-sustaining. The garden could be seen in the same way. Farmers, gardeners, animals, manure, crops, plants, soil, compost—as well as celestial bodies—all comprise a distinct and thriving ecosystem.

Lunar cycles influence plant growth in some surprising ways. Experiments have shown that seed germination and plant growth hasten when the moon is waxing. This means the days leading up to the full moon are best for planting and sowing seeds (especially ones that yield an aboveground harvest). It is thought that the stronger gravitational force of the moon pulls the water up from the ground, providing more moisture for seeds and roots. When the moon is waning, it is a good time to plant flowering bulbs, perennials, and root vegetables. The days leading up to the new moon are a time for rest, ideal for weeding and trimming.

In fact, some believe that not only the lunar phases but also the zodiac sign the moon is in has an effect on plant growth. The best time to plant leaf crops is when the moon is in the water signs of Scorpio, Pisces, and Cancer, whereas root crops are best planted in the earth signs of Virgo, Capricorn, and Taurus. Flowers should be planted in the air signs of Gemini, Libra, and Aquarius, and fruits in the fire signs of Leo, Sagittarius, and Aries.

Even if you don't garden with the phases of the moon, part of appreciating your own moon garden is being in touch with the moon's cycles and its powers.

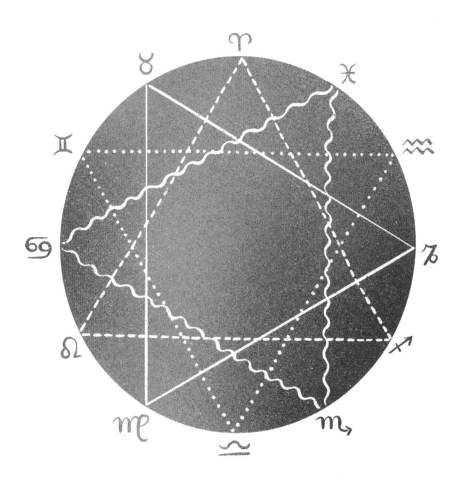

FIRE (fruit)   - - - - - - - - -
AIR (flower)   · · · · · · · · · · · ·
WATER (leaf)   ∿∿∿∿
EARTH (root)   ━━━━━

DESIGNING YOUR MOON GARDEN

Enjoying a moon garden can be an unexpectedly sensual experience. It relies less on the sight of vibrant, colorful displays, and more on the soft glow of white flowers, the nocturnal pollinators drawn to their luminescence, the scents of night-blooming plants, and the sounds of nature that resound in the stillness of the night.

When designing a moon garden, it's important to keep certain elements in mind. Combining varying textures, forms, and silhouettes, a moon garden can be a lush and evocative assortment of flowers, grasses, vines, shrubs, and trees. The palette is a spectrum of lighter colors—whites, ivories, pale yellows, lavenders, and silvers—that are most reflective under the starry night sky. Fragrant plants like jasmine, honeysuckle, and nicotiana, with their aromas wafting through the garden in intoxicating bursts, can add to the holistic experience of the garden.

This chapter will guide you through the process of creating your evening oasis. First, we'll explore general design principles with a focus on backyard gardens, stylistic elements that will elevate your space, and tips for creating a habitat garden attractive to wildlife. Then we'll look at creating moon gardens for small spaces like rooftops and terraces as well as indoor container gardens.

Design Principles

Designing a moon garden is a process of alchemy: location, layout, texture, color, and fragrance all culminate in a luminous vision. We'll explore how these elements work together, whether you're planting in a backyard, on a rooftop, indoors, or in a window box.

LOCATION

When choosing a location for your moon garden, look for a plot under the open sky, avoiding dense tree canopies or other obstructions that could block the moonlight. This will also make for the best stargazing. In a larger yard where you have options and can choose a dedicated area for your moon garden, consider a spot close to your house. Not only will you have enchanting views of the garden from inside the house, but you'll be able to enjoy the scents of night-fragrant plants wafting in through your windows. Plus, many night-blooming plants are tropical and potted in containers, so keeping them close by gives you easy access for watering. On a rooftop, you're in luck—you will likely have unobstructed views of the night sky but may need to shelter more fragile flowering plants from gusty winds. If you're creating an indoor moon garden, you'll want to carve out an area near your window where the moonlight streams in.

Lighting Key

●	FULL SUN	needs at least six hours of direct sunlight each day.
◑	PARTIAL SUN	needs four to six hours of direct sun, leaning toward more sun rather than less.
◔	PARTIAL SHADE	needs four to six hours of direct sun, preferring to be sheltered from afternoon sun.
⊜	FULL SHADE	needs less than four hours of direct sun, or dappled shade all day.

SITE ANALYSIS

Your garden design will be influenced by the conditions of your space. These help inform what kind of plants you can grow in your garden. Once you've zeroed in on a space for your garden, the first step is to take note of the following factors; in gardening and landscaping speak, we call this the "site analysis."

Light

Paradoxically, perhaps the biggest consideration when planning your moon garden is . . . the sun. Although you'll be enjoying your garden in the evening, the plants will still be growing during the day, so you need to be mindful of the amount of sunlight your garden receives.

First, observe the sunlight in your chosen space throughout the day. What areas get full sun, part sun or part shade, or full shade? What areas are blasted by direct afternoon sunlight? How does the light shift throughout the day?

Now imagine how the sun "travels" throughout the year. The sun's angle seems to shift as the earth tilts toward and away from it through the seasons. In the Northern Hemisphere, the sun travels lowest across the sky in the months around the winter solstice and highest in the months around the summer solstice. This means that any neighboring obstructions like tree canopies and tall buildings may cast a shadow on your space when the sun is at a lower angle and not when the sun is higher in the sky.

Once you have a sense of the sunlight in your space, look for plants that will thrive in your space. When shopping, check plant tags to determine their light preferences (see Lighting Key on page 27).

Soil

If you're planting your moon garden in the ground, assess the soil conditions and characteristics. Is the soil rich and fertile, sandy, or clay? Are there a lot of earthworms? You may need to add soil amendments like topsoil and compost to make your soil more suitable for planting. If you're planting a moon garden in containers or indoors, you can buy your preferred potting soil at the store.

Drainage

Observe the drainage in your outdoor space. After it rains, are there puddles or areas that remain muddy or boggy? If you have boggier conditions, you will want to choose plants that like to stay moist.

Wind

How windy is your space? In an urban backyard you may not get much wind or airflow because of surrounding buildings. But on the penthouse terrace of an apartment building, the winds may be powerful. Check which direction the prevailing winds come from. Many plants don't fare well in cold winter winds or hot summer winds, but other plants, like arborvitaes, can act as a windscreen.

GARDEN LAYOUT

When considering the layout of your moon garden, think about how you want to experience it. Is there a natural path? Where is a comfortable place to sit? Will you primarily use the space for dining or entertaining, or do you intend to fill it with plants? Designate areas for seating, a walkway, containers, and garden beds, if applicable.

Here's where it can be helpful to make a plan that's roughly to scale. One option is to take measurements of your space and draw the plan on grid-lined paper, where each square represents one foot. Add any existing trees, structures, vents, or anything else that will influence the rest of your design. This is your foundational plan. Draw the new structural elements you would like to add, such as paths, hardscaping, arbors, and trellises. Next, add garden beds, planters, and plants. You don't have to know the exact varieties of plants you're going with yet, but think about the kind of growth structure you want them to have, such as upright, spreading, climbing, arching, or crawling—and roughly sketch them in. (To visualize different configurations, draw various layouts on tracing paper placed over your foundational plan.)

If you already have an existing garden, you can integrate moon garden elements. Add flowering white and night-fragrant plants throughout garden beds, for example, or devote a section of your garden specifically to your moon palette. In a large garden, you can create smaller "rooms" like Vita Sackwell-West's, bordered by grasses or evergreen hedges, to create an intimate space for an enchanting night garden.

If you have a wall that you can use for your garden, consider incorporating it into your layout. Walls can offer protection and shade from direct sunlight, a great reprieve for white flowers that can quickly wilt in the hot afternoon sun. Walls also offer structural support for trellises and climbing vines like honeysuckle and clematis, creating opportunities for more lushness and fragrance.

LAYERING YOUR PLANTS

With a basic layout of your garden space completed, begin to consider how you might fill it. In general, you want to create layers of plants—layering creates depth and movement, which in turn offer a more immersive experience. Imagine how all the plants will move and sway together when the wind blows.

Start with the structural layer, comprising the plants that give a garden its general outline; this layer serves as a backbone for other ornamental plants. If you're working against a wall or a fence, the structural layer will likely run along its interior edges. Evergreen shrubs or trees like boxwoods, ilexes, rhododendrons, and yews are great for a structural layer, especially as they remain green year-round. Deciduous shrubs and trees work well too, and even when their branches are bare, their distinctive bark color and flower seed heads can offer winter interest.

Once you establish the structure, build out from there. The second layer, the midsection, is essential for giving shape to the garden and should consist of flowering perennials, woody shrubs, biennials, and annuals. Use a mix of colors, forms, and textures to add drama and contrast, such as ornamental grasses with their feathery plumes, rounded hydrangeas, and the tall spires of foxgloves.

The front layer, or border, comprises border plantings—
usually shorter plants with a mounded or crawling growth
habit—along with spring bulbs like tulips and snowdrops.
You can add multiple front layers depending on how much
space you have.

Layering adds visual interest and helps give the garden
a rich dimensionality. To visualize layering, think of a class

CONSIDER THE HISTORY

Your garden may have a long and interesting history of its own before you came to live there. If it is an old property, there are likely plants and trees that were planted by families generations ago or that settled there via wind and seed. If there is an old tree in your yard, imagine all that tree has experienced and endured in its life, the fruit it has borne and the animals it has fed, the shade its canopy has offered to understory plants, animals, and residents who preceded you. Build a relationship with this tree and honor it; it can be a key element of your garden design.

If you don't have old trees or shrubs, you have the opportunity to choose new specimens and start shaping a new story for your garden. A new tree can be a focal point, accompanied by understory plants and ground cover. Some tree specimens perfect for a moon garden are dogwoods, viburnum, and magnolias.

photo with the tallest kids in the back, shorter kids in front of them, and a front row of kids kneeling. Everyone is staggered so you can see each person's face. Layering with plants is not that different—generally speaking, you want the plants that grow the tallest farther back and the shorter plants in front. Staggering them offers an organic flow and ensures none of them are hidden from view.

For the most drama and impact, collect each plant in a group rather than planting a one-off (e.g., plant several rosemary bushes in one area rather than a single rosemary bush). There is strength in numbers. This *mass planting* technique lends a sense of lushness and abundance and yields the most luminescence.

Layer plants in containers in the same way, placing the smallest containers with the shortest plants in front so you can see the foliage of all the plants behind. Group containers in threes or fives; odd numbers appear more natural than pairs.

As you plan your garden, imagine not only how the garden looks now and the current scale of the plants, but also how it will look five years from now when the plants are grown, sprinkled with buds, then opening flowers, and finally seed heads, with birds nesting among their dense branches.

TEXTURE AND FORM

Whether your night garden is planted indoors or outdoors, the play of texture and form is integral. Many leaf attributes, like size, shape, color, and surface texture—smooth or rough, glossy or matte—influence how the light hits them and how we perceive them.

Fine-textured plants with needle- or thread-like leaves, like amsonia and lavender, offer a light, breezy impression. They can make small spaces feel more airy and spacious. Plants with bigger, broader leaves (and/or flowers), like hostas, alocasias, and rhododendrons, can have a more dominating presence in broad daylight—think of them as statement plants. As the light fades, however, these bold plants can double as a strong backdrop for your nightly show of moon garden flowers. Part of the fun when choosing plants is curating unique arrangements with varying textures and forms to create a dynamic, attractive garden.

COLOR

The moon garden palette consists of whites, silver, grays, greens, and yellows, as these shades shine brightest in the moonlight. Whereas darker colors like red and forest green absorb light, white and pale hues reflect it, creating a luminous glow in the darkness.

White is the brightest color at night by far. Though it may sound plain, there are actually so many different shades of white—whites with warmer and cooler undertones, and hues like arctic white, ecru, dove, and ivory. And among white flowers, plenty feature painted strokes and splashes of other colors—the yellow centers of bunchflower daffodils, the "black eye" of white anemones, the pink-dipped petals of the regal lily. These touches of color add charm and character to a moon garden.

Silver and grays shimmer in plants like dusty miller and silver nickel vine, lustrous against the blanket of night. At twilight, the icy gray cotton lavender artemisia transforms into low silver hills. Plants that gleam come nightfall add an ethereal, almost magical quality to any moon garden. In Scottish folklore, a silver branch covered in white blossoms can transport you into the fairy world.

Shades of green are important in adding depth and dimension. A darker green background, often provided by evergreen shrubs like boxwoods, rhododendrons, and yews, contrasts with light-colored flowers, allowing them to pop in the darkness.

For instance, the creamy white flowers of a sweetbay magnolia shine against its glossy green leaves. Blending different shades of green foliage softens the contrast between the darker greenery and the much lighter floral hues.

It may surprise you how brightly yellow can stand out in dusk and darkness. A hazy glow radiates from yellow flowers at night, almost like a lingering memento of the setting sun. Planted in a border, the creamy yellow ruffles of the Tulip 'Verona' could even illuminate a garden path under the full moon. This color, traditionally associated with friendship, transforms into an even warmer tone at night.

Variegated plants with two-toned foliage of white and green or yellow and green are also visible in the darkness. Try *Aeonium arboreum* 'Luteovariegatum' (a rosette-shaped succulent) or the 'Silver King' Euonymus (a dense evergreen shrub).

Pale pink, purple, and blue flowers all add beauty to a moon garden. While they won't pop like white flowers, their hints of color will enhance the overall mood at night as well as brighten your garden in the daytime. Of course, if you are inclined to add brighter, bolder colors like fuchsia or crimson red for daytime drama, don't hold back—just remember that these colors will not be as visible in the darkness.

FRAGRANCE

In the evening, as the light wanes and our vision diminishes, it's almost as if our sense of smell grows stronger. We begin to rely less on sight and engage our other senses more, which changes how we experience and connect with our environment.

The fragrance of night-blooming flowers animates a garden from dusk to dawn and heightens the senses, luring us closer. Night-blooming plants are especially fragrant because they rely heavily on their aromas to attract nocturnal pollinators like moths and bats. Many day-blooming plants continue to be very fragrant into the evening—for example, lilacs, peonies, and, in spite of their name, daylilies.

Flowers release many different types of scents to attract their pollinators—some sweet, some spicy, some musky, and some, like that of the stapelia flower, downright rotten.

Fragrance preference is very personal; a smell that one person loves might be nauseating to another. The scent of night-blooming jasmine (*Cestrum nocturnum*) is just one example—it's dripping with sweetness, and for some it might be too much of a good thing. In general, it's best to avoid planting two plant varieties with disparate powerful scents right next to each other. This can quickly turn into sensory overload. (Ever felt nauseous in a candle store or after trying a bunch of perfume samples?)

When choosing the placement of plants, have some fun mapping out an aroma guide for your garden. You may have enjoyed stopping and smelling each plant in an aroma garden, rubbing the leaves to release their scent and bringing your nose down to the flowers. What sweet smells would you like to greet you in your garden? Plant those plants in a container or train them up an entryway wall. Other scents can envelop you as you meander along a path or recline in a chair under the stars.

If you don't know where to start—perhaps your city nose is more acquainted with a bakery's aroma of freshly baked bread or the unpleasant odors of trash night—visit a nursery and roam the aisles, acquainting yourself with various plants and their scents. Snap some pictures of your favorites for reference (with their labels facing you to catch their names and prices) and take note of their fragrance. Some plants are poisonous, either in part or in their entirety, so do your research before bringing them home, and be mindful of the varieties you choose for highly trafficked areas where children or pets play. Nurseries are a wonderful resource, but you can also simply walk around your neighborhood, stopping to smell the proverbial (and literal!) roses.

Pink jasmine (*Jasminum polyanthum*) is a popular choice and a lovely option to plant near entrances or walkways. Its sweet perfume is light and not overpowering. Jasmine vines are natural climbers, covering and draping over fences in an elegant fashion. Honeysuckle is another perfumed climbing plant—perfect for a trellis near a seating area since it is not only fragrant both day and night but also attracts humming-birds and moths.

When you bring these fragrant plants home, stage them in the spots you have in mind and do a walk-through at night. The perennials will likely not all be in bloom, so use your imagination when necessary. Make sure the scents intermingle pleasantly and are not overwhelming in any one area. (Also, check that the plants are suited to the light exposure in those locations.)

THE SCENT OF STAPELIA

In my early days
of indoor gardening, I
propagated a stapelia plant
from a cutting. At the time, I
was unaware of stapelia's beautiful
blooms; I was simply drawn to the soft,
fuzzy cactus leaves. Excited and proud when
the propagation was a success, I was elated
when it bloomed one day in October three
years later. The flower was covered in fine
hairs that resembled fur, and its scent was
of rotting meat. Stapelia takes on the
characteristics of a corpse to attract
pollinators like blowflies. By day
four, flies were swarming outside
my window, trying to get in
on the action!

Garden Elements

Your garden is more than the plants that grow in it—it's a
vibescape you're creating. The following sections will help you
think about the atmosphere and ambience you want to achieve
through elements like lighting, water features, and seating.

LIGHTING

Fairy lights, lanterns, and candles all add to the mystical nighttime mood of a moon garden, illuminating both plants and
paths, especially on darker nights. This kind of soft lighting
subtly guides you and your guests along so you can immerse
yourselves in the silvery light and wafting scents.

    When designing with lights, consider the locals who also
live in your backyard—the insects, birds, and nocturnal wildlife. Bright nighttime lighting is too jarring for a moon garden
and it also contributes to light pollution, which disrupts the
natural circadian rhythms in both humans and animals. This
brightened night sky or "sky glow" disorients animals (like
migratory birds) that rely on the moon and stars as their
guides. Moths, the primary pollinators of night-blooming
plants, and other pollinating insects are very attracted to

artificial light and often die upon contact with it. (These insects serve as food to birds, and without this food source, bird populations are also at risk.) Sky glow is also what makes it difficult for modern urbanites to see the stars at night.

When lighting your moon garden, let an ecological approach inform your design decisions. The color, strength, and direction of the lighting you choose will make a difference to the local habitat. Studies have shown that amber and yellow lights are far less disruptive to wildlife than blue and ultraviolet lights, which attract moths. So stick to those warmer yellows. We, too, are drawn to the blue light emitted from our phones and computer screens! And just as blue light is detrimental to moths, in humans it can lower the production of melatonin, which our bodies produce when it's dark; less melatonin pro-duction is connected to fatigue, stress, and sleep disturbance. Keep outdoor lighting soft and minimal, direct your lights toward the ground rather than pointing them toward the sky, and turn them off when you are not using them.

In addition to lighting pathways, illuminate steps and any elevation changes to avoid stumbling. Fairy lights and LED bulb lights strung along fences add a soft glow to the plants below, and when placed above seating and dining areas they enhance romantic moonlit dinners and nighttime festivities. Lanterns on tables and on the ground near lounge areas, door-ways, and planters offer gentle, diffused light and can illumi-nate potted plants. Orb-like lanterns evoke the full moon in the garden. Hanging lightweight lanterns from tree branches adds an extra touch of magic; you can make your own with papier-mâché, or decorate paper lanterns with embellish-ments like pressed flowers and leaves. Solar-powered lights are energy efficient and convenient but need enough sunlight during the day to power them at night.

Indoors, keep lighting soft and minimal as well. Place lanterns on the floor near potted plants and seating areas.

Candleholders with cutouts scatter the light in ways that can mimic the night sky. Adorn mantels and other surfaces with candles and flickering tea lights to evoke fireflies dancing around your indoor garden.

WATER FEATURES

Integrating a water feature into a moon garden enhances its serenity. The sound of trickling water is infinitely soothing, especially at night when all is quiet except for croaking toads and chirping crickets. In an urban landscape, it's an antidote to street noise. Water reflects the glimmering moonlight, emphasizing its glow. And however small the source, water creates a feeling of movement and circulation within the garden, making the space feel larger.

A babbling brook or stream nearby is a dream feature in a moon garden. But for most of us, a fountain will work wonders to recreate the sounds of nature. It can be simple— a recirculating wall fountain with a basin is great for smaller spaces like terraces and decks. It requires an electric pump to circulate the water and a power source to plug it in. You can feature a smaller fountain inside your home too; even a table-top-sized water basin or trickling rock fountain is profoundly relaxing. Be sure to check the weight of any feature before committing—cast stone can be very heavy.

If you have a pond, consider adding lotuses and tropical water lilies, many of which are night blooming, very fragrant, and come in white and light yellows, pinks, and purples. For those without a pond, a steel galvanized tub makes a quick water feature that can work in any size garden. Make it a focal point, surrounded by leafy foliage, and add floating candles or fresh-cut blossoms for a little extra romance (gardenias and orchids float, for example). Leave enough room in the vessel so the moon's reflection can be seen on its surface. (And remember to refresh the water regularly to prevent standing water from attracting mosquitoes.)

To recreate this on a smaller scale indoors, fill a wide, shallow bowl with water and add cut flowers—a single magnolia blossom floating in a bowl adds a peaceful quality to an indoor moonscape.

Bird baths not only attract birds to sip and bathe, but they can also serve as a classic water feature. Position the bird bath in the open so predators can't sneak up unseen and so you can enjoy the views of birds visiting.

SEATING

How would you like to spend time in your garden at night? Maybe you seek a quiet space to think—or the opposite, a space to release yourself from thoughts. Your garden offers many different uses: It can be a place of contemplation or relaxation, or an intimate, casual setting to catch up with a friend, host dinner parties, or stargaze. Consider seating and furniture that will work for the occasions you plan to use it for the most. This could mean a daybed or a hammock for lounging, a couple of Adirondack chairs, a dining table and chairs, or all of these, depending on the size and layout of your space (and budget!). I'm partial to a classic wooden garden bench for its simplicity and utility; made of natural material, it offers a quiet place for reflection. Your chosen seating will of course influence your garden's overall look and feel. Whether it be a bench or a boulder, these elements offer both a visual focal point and a place to rest, so choose attractive, pleasing pieces.

When investing in outdoor furniture, think of your region's weather patterns—if it rains all the time, for example, chairs of recycled plastic or metal can withstand the elements. Weather-treated wood furniture is hardy as well and will last longer outdoors when covered to protect it from sun, rain, and general moisture.

For an indoor moon garden, designate a seating area near a window where moonlight streams in and you have a view of the night sky. Envelop your space with lush plants of varying heights. Position your favorite lounge chair or other furniture amid this greenery so you feel nestled into a distinctly natural space. Whether you're absorbed in a book, listening to music, or meditating, reserve this nook for soaking up the restful energies of the moon, reconnecting with yourself, and appreciating the garden you've cultivated.

Native Species and Local Wildlife

Native plant species play an integral role in supporting wildlife and a biodiverse ecosystem. We are at a point in the climate crisis where part of being a good gardener means good stewardship of the land you are cultivating, however small it may be. Your moon garden can be a source of sustenance, replenishment, and resilience for native plant and wildlife species (like birds, bees, butterflies, moths, and bats), contributing to collective and interconnected well-being. Working intentionally with your bioregion's ecosystem can give you and your moon garden a surprisingly tangible and rewarding sense of purpose.

We live in a culture that is overall very bug-phobic, thinking of insects in general as pests that should be eradicated. It's time to destigmatize bugs! We need to embrace and protect many insect species because they play a crucial role in the health of the ecosystem. The health of birds relies on the health of bugs. So if you love having birds visiting, singing, and fluttering in your garden, lead the way by creating a habitat-rich and inviting garden that mimics and amplifies your natural local bioregion.

The next chapter suggests many region-specific native plants you can incorporate into your moon garden. But beyond that, I encourage you to research plants native to your region (and learn what's invasive, so you can avoid planting those). Create a sanctuary not only for yourself but for local flora and fauna too. There are many more plants not covered in this book that would work perfectly in a moon garden.

ATTRACTING WILDLIFE TO YOUR MOON GARDEN

Research the local wildlife and see what birds, insects, reptiles, amphibians, and small mammals are native to your area. By taking their preferences into consideration, you can create a beautiful, sustainable garden teeming with life.

Fireflies, which live mainly east of the Rockies, look like low-lying stars as they flash their lights in the summer night sky. Their bioluminescent bellies emit a yellow-green glow, giving these beetles another name—lightning bugs. The flickering patterns that spark childlike surprise and wonder are specific to each species, designed to attract mates. When they're in their larval stage as glowworms, they support your garden's health by eating slugs and snails. To attract more fireflies into your garden, grow a diversity of native plants, avoid mowing grass and raking up leaf litter (the larvae live in the grass), add a water feature, and keep garden lights low.

If you love hummingbirds in your garden in the daytime, then you will also love hawk moths in your night garden. Hawk moths are very large and birdlike, hence their name; they're also known as hummingbird moths. Hovering over flowers, flapping their wings rapidly (they can fly up to 30 miles [48 km] per hour!), and using their long strawlike tongues to drink nectar, they pollinate many night-blooming and native plants.

Bats eat mosquitos, which is only one reason to love them. Bats pollinate many nocturnal flowers, drawn to those with muskier and spicier scents. You'll see bats flying and swooping after dusk, looking for food and to mate.

CASE STUDY:

SANTA CRUZ DESERT MOON GARDEN

While planning my sister's terrace moon garden in Santa Cruz, size and scale were important considerations. Space was limited: there was already a surfboard, a table, a huge succulent visited by a ruby-throated Anna's hummingbird, and a wandering toddler.

The terrace is sun-drenched, with an adobe-colored stucco wall. Because Northern California is unfortunately in a perpetual drought, I opted for drought-tolerant plants. Plants that need less frequent watering, like succulents, put less strain on local resources. Succulents can survive on little water because they store water in their leaves, hence their plump and adorable appearance.

Given the amount of light, the color of the walls, and the environmental conditions, we went with a desert aesthetic for the moon garden, with night-blooming cactus, silvery-gray succulents like silver dollar jade and agave, and native California plants like white sage [*Salvia apiana*]. I added a sweetly scented pink jasmine to vine laterally along her fence, and a white passionflower vine to climb a wooden trellis. For planters, we used a collection of whitewashed terra-cotta in varying sizes and shapes, including a large cylinder, a couple with rounded bottoms, and a short, low bowl. Even though my sister looked longingly at the nursery's magnolia tree saplings, it wasn't going to happen—they would soon outgrow her little terrace.

Moon Gardens for Small Spaces

Designing a garden for a small space is an artful endeavor with both perks and challenges. The following sections cover design ideas and practical considerations when creating a moon garden in a smaller space, be it on a terrace or rooftop, in a window box, or in your home.

TERRACE AND ROOFTOP MOON GARDENS

A terrace, balcony, or rooftop is an elevated extension of the home where you can create an open-air living room. Weight and access are important considerations, but you eliminate some other challenges—like deer potentially eating your plants.

Think about how you want to use your moon garden at night: What kind of furniture suits that purpose, and where will it go? Orient your seating for the best view of the stars and sky. Be sure to leave enough space between the furniture and planters so you can move freely around the garden. As you plan for larger elements like shrubs and trees, make sure they won't block your view; instead, use them to frame it! Take measurements and make a plan, as outlined on page 29.

When choosing a plant palette for a rooftop or terrace garden, first do an assessment of your environmental conditions. Is it in full sun or does an overhang or an overhead tree offer shade? Is it very windy, and if so, are certain areas more protected? Avoid planting delicate flowers or plants that won't fare well in gusty conditions.

For a container garden on a ground level patio, you don't have to worry as much about wind or weight, but there may be less light and air circulation if it is surrounded by trees or tall buildings, so choose your plants accordingly.

For a terrace, rooftop, or balcony garden where you can't plant directly in the ground, choose plants that grow well in containers—there are many perennials, shrubs, and some trees that grow well in pots. In the ground, plants' roots can spread freely in search of moisture and nutrients. A pot has strict limits. To support a long life span, choose containers large enough for your new plants (and their roots) to grow into— this is especially important for trees. Different plants require different size pots, so do a little research or consult a nursery employee. Rectangular and round planters both have appeal, depending on how much space you have to work with and the aesthetic you are going for. You can line the terrace perimeter with rectangular planters to save square footage and maximize planting space. Wider planters allow for more planting depth and opportunities for layering, and they have a sleek, contemporary look.

Round planters offer flexibility in styling with more varied shapes and sizes. Rolled-rim terra-cotta and brushed antique planters fit an old-world, classical style; smooth fiberglass planters look more modern.

Try combining both styles: For example, a row of rectangular planters with evergreen shrubs or ornamental grasses creates a lush, green backdrop behind a couch. (If the seating area is protected from wind, try plants like boxwoods with

lavender; if it's more open and airy, try grasses like fountain grass or muhly). Then layer round planters of varying sizes on either end of the couch to frame and envelop it in flora. Larger round planters can host fragrant white flowering shrubs like summersweet and hydrangea; medium-sized planters are perfect for silver-toned foliage plants or flowering perennials like false indigo (*Baptisia alba*) and beardtongue (*Penstemon digitalis*); and smaller planters can be filled with white and yellow annuals like nicotiana and nemesia. Try a silver-toned annual like licorice plant (*Helichrysum petiolare*) spilling out of one of the planters. Install a trellis on a neighboring wall with a climbing vine of potted moonflower or honeysuckle.

A tree will bring height and structure to a terrace garden. You won't want to bring home any varieties that will grow too huge (like a magnolia or an oak tree). Many large trees also come in more compact varieties, so if there's a certain plant you absolutely love and know would bring you joy—but worry it would grow too huge—look for a miniature version. Japanese maples and river birches grow well in containers, and river birches can typically withstand the harsh light and windy conditions on rooftops. Evergreen trees like arborvitaes and junipers work well too.

Consider how much weight you are putting on your terrace. If you have an older home or plan to put a lot of plant material on your terrace, consult a structural engineer. Soil retains water, and wet soil adds weight to the planter. To help manage weight concerns, go easy on the trees (do your research before bringing home even a small tree), and opt for lightweight planters. Fiberglass planters are a light option and also long-lasting and frost resistant. If you live in a cold region, it's important to get frost-resistant planters—residual water in planters can freeze during the winter and cause cracks.

Because your moon garden will consist of mostly white and light-colored plants, complement this palette with planter colors in the midtone range. Earth tones like terracotta, taupe, and stone gray; natural materials like wood; and weathering steel that weathers into a rich rust color over time would be beautiful. Black planters are stylish—they provide a stark, higher-contrast look with an upscale vibe. They pair well with both evergreens and silver foliage, and they hide dirt easily. However, black planters can sometimes make a space feel smaller, whereas white planters can help a smaller space feel more open and airy. But white planters will compete with the white flowers and silver foliage, and in the daylight you might find all that white piercingly bright. It's all personal preference, but midtones are a safe bet, as they blend well with the moon garden palette both day and night. You'll want to complement the existing materials of the flooring, fencing, and walls. And you can make alterations to your existing space too; for example, maybe you want to paint your fence a darker, moodier color for more drama, or throw down some outdoor rugs to make your space even cozier.

Window Boxes

When it comes to planting window boxes and containers, use the age-old recipe of thriller + filler + spiller to create a beautiful mini moon garden in any container.

The thriller catches the eye; it's the statement plant that the rest of the container is designed around. Plants with showy flowers and/or brilliant foliage, like angelonias, mulla mulla, and caladiums, make great thrillers. Your thriller may also be tall (like gaura) and thus offer structure to the overall design as well.

A filler adds body to the arrangement and fills the empty spaces around the thriller. It plays a supporting role, helping the arrangement feel abundant and cohesive. You can have more than one kind of filler. Their texture, leaf size, and color should be different from yet complementary to the thriller's; for example, euphorbia 'White Sparkle' makes a great filler for a caladium thriller. Other good fillers are dwarf evergreens, dusty miller, and white pansies.

The spiller plant cascades, or spills, out of the planter to give the arrangement whimsy, romance, and an almost effervescent sense of abundance. Include several different varieties of spillers. For example, one trailing vine with larger leaves

SAMPLE PLANT PALETTES

FOR SEASONAL MOON GARDENS IN YOUR WINDOW BOXES

EARLY SPRING ⚙

THRILLER	Bulbs like daffodils, tulips, and hyacinths
FILLER	Pansies, nemesia, asparagus fern
SPILLER	Variegated vinca vine

LATE SPRING/SUMMER ☀

THRILLER	Lavender, gaura, or caladium
FILLER	*Euphorbia hypericifolia* 'Stardust White sparkle'
SPILLER	Variegated vinca vine with silver nickel vine

FALL 🍃

THRILLER	Heuchera [any silver-toned variety], cyclamen, ornamental cabbage 'Osaka White'; add in white pumpkins and gourds to taste
FILLER	Dwarf arborvitaes or dwarf boxwoods
SPILLER	Variegated ivy*

WINTER ❄

THRILLER	Heuchera, heather [*Calluna vulgaris*], and ornamental cabbage
FILLER	Dwarf arborvitaes or dwarf boxwoods
SPILLER	Variegated ivy*

*NOTE: Ivy is invasive in some areas; use only in the fall and winter and discard before their berries arrive in spring and birds can spread their seed.

and a second with smaller leaves; or a leafy vine complement-
ing a flowering vine can make the flowers seem extra decadent. Some good spillers are variegated vinca vine, silver nickel
vine, and creeping phlox.

Generally speaking, small flowering annuals are best for
window boxes because you can rotate them out seasonally
and they're inexpensive. You can also buy them in small sizes,
which is ideal for the limited space of a window box.

It is tempting when the first warm day rolls around in
March to go out and buy plants for your window boxes. But it
can be risky to plant too early; one subsequent cold night can
freeze freshly planted flowers and undo a day's worth of hard
work. In early spring, be sure to plant only flowers that are
cold-hardy in your region.

Depending on how cold your region gets, many fall window
box plants can survive throughout the winter. So if you want to
save money or time, choose a winter-hardy design for your fall
boxes.

Indoor Moon Gardens

Outdoor space isn't always an option; especially in cities, it can be a rare luxury. Fortunately, many tropical plants that are kept outdoors in the summertime can be grown indoors year-round. Your indoor garden can invite the moon's energy and be a magical space regardless of the season and freezing nighttime temperatures.

When creating an indoor moon garden, carve out an area closest to your windows where you have a view of the moon and the night sky. If you can't see the sky, don't worry. You can create the right atmosphere by using soft mood lighting and designing a lush, intimate space with silver-leaved, light-reflective plants and fragrance from blooms, candles, or incense. Feel free to call this space your sunroom *and* your moon room!

EMULATING THE WILD

When growing plants indoors, try to replicate the conditions of their natural environment—light, water, and humidity—as much as possible. For example, a night-blooming cereus hails from Mexico and loves sunlight; to grow it indoors, hang it

HOW TO

FORCE PAPERWHITES INDOORS

1 Choose a wide, shallow glass bowl or vessel without drainage holes.

2 Lay 1 to 2 inches [2.5 to 5 cm] of clean pebbles or marbles in the bottom of the vessel. These will help keep the bulbs upright and in position.

3 Add a layer of bulbs, pointed sides up, and fit them snugly together so they can support each other and you get a multitude of blooms. Fill in the empty areas between the bulbs with more pebbles, keeping the top third of the bulbs exposed.

4 Fill the vessel with tap water just so the bottoms of the bulbs are barely sitting in water. [Do not submerge the bulbs; they may rot.]

5 Keep the bulbs in a cool, shady spot [50° to 60°F/10° to 15°C] while they root. Check the water levels regularly and add water when necessary.

6 Once you see roots, move the vessel to a sunny spot, ideally near a window or on a windowsill. Avoid heaters or warm areas.

7 Witness these beauties bloom! The paperwhites will bloom for up to 2 weeks. For longer-lasting blooms, move them to a spot with less direct light. Group several bowls of these flowers together by a window and notice how they gleam in the moonlight and exude a sweet fragrance.

in a window that receives a lot of light, ideally south-facing. In the wild, staghorn ferns are *epiphytic*, meaning they grow on trees, not in soil, so indoors they're happiest mounted on wooden plaques on a wall. Many houseplant species hail from tropical rainforests and have evolved in very humid climates. Regularly misting your plants, running a humidifier, and placing your plants upon a water-filled tray of pebbles can raise the humidity levels in your garden. Tropical plants also like to be grouped together as a family because they raise each other's humidity levels.

SUNLIGHT AND SPACE

It can be challenging to give houseplants the sunlight they need when dealing with the practicalities of living in a small space with furniture and possessions. (One year I unsuccessfully tried to convince my partner that we should downsize our bed in order to make room for more plants.) Get a little creative! There's a lot of furniture that can support plants to maximize space—open shelving instead of closed cabinets, footstools as plant stands, mantels and nonworking fireplaces, or even stairs. Use stacks of books to elevate plants and display them at different heights near windows. (Just avoid radiators or heaters in the wintertime—these can fry your plants! Similarly, keep plants away from air-conditioning drafts, which can damage leaves.)

Using a compass (there's likely one on your phone), or by observing the rising and setting sun, determine which direction(s) your windows face. This dictates the intensity of the natural light streaming into your home. South-facing light is the brightest and most direct throughout the day. It is great for growing sun-loving plants such as ficus varieties, succulents, and cacti. North-facing light is softer and less direct throughout the day, with an ambient, diffused quality.

While north-facing rooms can get some direct light in the morning and in the late afternoon, plants that enjoy some shade will grow best in north-facing light. East-facing light is brightest in the morning, and west-facing light is brightest in the late afternoon.

Consider any obstructions to your light; tree canopies and any construction or scaffolding can block the light coming in through your windows. Lastly, consider what floor you live on: North-facing light will be much softer on the ground floor than on the twenty-fifth floor.

LAYER, LAYER, LAYER

Most of the design principles we've discussed apply to an indoor garden, particularly layering. An evergreen hedge is not viable indoors, but you can create a dense green backdrop using larger plants with broad green leaves as well as plants with smaller, compact leaves. Some good options include cultivars of the rubber plant (*Ficus elastica*) with thick burgundy leaves; the fiddle-leaf fig tree or bush (*Ficus lyrata*) with its dark green, fiddle-shaped leaves; the Norfolk Island pine or *Dracaena* 'Lisa' for height and structure; palms; and bushier trees like the umbrella tree (a choice cultivar is *Schefflera actinophylla* 'Amate'). You could also create a dense green layer with several ZZ plants (*Zamioculcas zamiifolia*) and/or a variety of snake plants (*Dracaena zeylanica* or *trifasciata*) elevated at different heights with stands (snake plants take up the least amount of space). This backdrop acts like blue velvet behind your "jewels": Place your moon garden plants with white flowers and silver or variegated foliage in front of these larger plants. Try incorporating orchids on small stands or side tables, their blooming stems adding arcs of white or yellow.

VERTICALITY

One key element to creating an indoor garden oasis that feels
lush is verticality. Install plants on multiple levels—as if creating
a forest understory and canopy—and really surround yourself in
greenery from floor to ceiling. This gives the sense of the garden
being a world unto itself. Hanging cascading plants from the
ceiling will draw your eye upward—choose shimmery varieties
like *Scindapsus treubii* 'Moonlight' and variegated plants like
the *Hoya carnosa* 'Krimson Queen.' Install them at varying
heights to mimic nature. Air plants can be hung in glass orbs
or nestled in sculptural pieces of driftwood. Hang orchids and
other epiphytic plants like tillandsias and Spanish moss from
the branches of larger indoor trees, like fiddle-leaf fig trees or
Ficus benghalensis 'Audrey.'

MIXING IT UP

Repeating plant species can make a garden space feel cohesive, especially in a smaller space. For example, use several
potted snake plants or several dragon trees (dracaenas) as your
structural layer. But to avoid looking too monochromatic or
homogenous, have fun mixing plants with different foliage,
textures, and coloration. For example, snake plant leaves can
have silver and white stripes, zig zags, bright yellow lines
or soft creamy ones; they can be broad, short leaves or tall,
bamboo-like blades. Enjoy these details during the day, and
then witness their reflective elements at night. Ferns are great
for layering and variation; their fine textures can soften spaces,
giving the garden an otherworldly feel. Explore the many fern
varieties, then mix and match.

PROPAGATING PLANTS

Building up a plant collection
[especially quickly] can get costly,
but it doesn't have to be. One of
the joys of plant parenthood is
that you can propagate your plants
[or your friends' plants] for free!
All you need is some glass jars or
vessels, a clean pair of pruners,
and patience. There are many ways
to propagate plants, and methods
vary depending on the plant, but
in general you begin by making a
cut just below a leaf node. Snip
off some of its surrounding leaves,
place the cutting in a Mason jar of
water or a propagation tube, and
wait for it to grow roots. Once you
see a good amount of roots [like
fine hairs floating in the water],
transplant the cutting into soil.

WINTER BLOOMING

Winter is an especially important time for those of us living in cold regions to still feel connected to nature. Especially as February trudges on and we ache for spring, having a breath of plant life indoors is good for our mental health. With house-plants, we can continue cultivating our green thumbs and enjoy lush greenery in our homes.

Winter's also the time to force flowering bulbs indoors. Hyacinths, crocuses, and snowdrops all need to be chilled for eight to fifteen weeks beforehand to mimic their winter dormancy period. (You can also buy them prechilled.) Holiday favorites like paperwhites and amaryllis hail from warmer climates and do not need chilling.

Many tropical plants and cactuses bloom in the North American wintertime. Most want several hours of direct sun each day or at least six hours of bright, unobstructed light. (Tip: If you live in a lower-light space, like a garden apartment or basement, or maybe your windows face a courtyard, you can install grow lights and keep these sun-loving varieties. When you're out of town, set the lights on a timer so they turn on and off automatically.) Christmas cactus, a striking and popular tropical cactus, blooms with gorgeous white, pale pink, and yellow flowers in November and December—perfect for a moon garden. Tropical plants like white orchids, bromeliads, and hoyas bloom at different times of the year.

You can rely on silver foliage to shine when your flowering plants are not in bloom. Fortunately, there are many indoor plants with silver tones that tolerate lower light. *Scindapsus pictus* 'Exotica' is a personal favorite. Its thick silver-splattered leaves cascade down and look beautiful trailing from a hanging planter. Hang it near a window so it catches the moonlight. *Aglaonema* 'Silver Bay,' with huge silvery leaves, requires very little maintenance and is also low-light tolerant.

If you are feeling adventurous, consider painting your garden's walls a dark, rich color to really make the plants stand out. Think midnight blue, forest green, or dusky purple. An assortment of potted broad-leafed philodendrons, angel wing begonias, orchids, and candles against a night-conjuring hue would set the mood.

STYLING WITH INDOOR PLANTERS

As you build your garden, you'll be curating a collection of pottery. Choose pots that complement each other in color, shape, and form, in varying heights, to create a cohesive assortment that allows the foliage and flowers to shine. Keep in mind the aesthetic of your surrounding furniture and decor. Buying planters is an investment, so it may be helpful to first compile a physical or digital mood board with images of planters along with your existing plants, furniture, rugs, and other elements.

Gray, white, or black stoneware and other neutral colors let the plants take center stage. Terra-cotta is an excellent and affordable choice, as most tropical plants and succulents thrive in the permeable, breathable containment that unglazed terra-cotta provides. Terra-cotta also ages beautifully and develops a rich, earthy patina over time.

Planter shape, color, and texture can amplify the moon's presence with crescent and orb shapes, silvery gray and pearly white tones, gritty surfaces, and iridescent finishes.

For a minimalist aesthetic, choose pots with clean lines, like cylinders and bowls, and neutral colors. For a more bohemian vibe, terra-cottas, rattan baskets, and pops of color complement textured rugs and fabrics. For a wabi-sabi approach, embrace unglazed pots with imperfections, asymmetry, and cracks. If you are a lover of vintage and antiques, incorporate brass planters, urns, and iron stands. To find unique, one-of-a-kind planters, check out local ceramicists, nurseries, vintage shops, flea markets, and estate sales.

DRAINAGE AND WATERING

Ensure all your planters have adequate drainage by always buying planters with holes in them, and saucers to go underneath them to catch water. Plants need to be able to drain excess water so their roots and soil don't get root rot.

If your planter doesn't have a saucer, search thrift stores for vintage plates and tea saucers with decorative details or retro patterns—dishes you might not ordinarily choose for dining but are perfect for adding character to your potted garden. Don't be afraid to mismatch the colors of your saucers to your pots—enjoy the unusual and unique combinations. To protect the floor from scratches, add felt furniture pads to the bottoms of your planters or saucers.

Always feel the soil before you water to tell whether your plant is ready for water. In general, houseplants like their soil to be thoroughly quenched and then allowed to dry out again before the next watering. Different species like their soil to dry out or stay moist to varying degrees. (Houseplant tip: If your plant's leaves are visibly drooping, check the soil—it's probably dry, meaning your plant is thirsty!)

IF YOUR PLANTER DOESN'T HAVE A DRAINAGE HOLE

YOU HAVE THREE OPTIONS:

1 Leave the plant in its plastic grow pot until it needs repotting.

2 When potting, start with a layer of lava rocks in the planter bottom for a drainage layer.

3 Drill a hole in the bottom of the planter using a ceramic tile drill bit. [Wear a mask so as not to breathe in the clay dust.]

PLANTS FOR A MOON GARDEN

In making your moon garden your own, think of plants you love from your past or have positive associations or a launching point from which the rest of your garden takes shape. These can act as inspiration or with flowers that spark joy, or new plants that fill you with wonder.

Your moon garden should consist of a mix of night bloomers, annuals, zone-hardy perennials, shrubs, and trees that bloom at different times of year. This ensures you'll have a botanical show each season with flowers opening in spring, summer, fall, and even winter. Perennials, shrubs, and trees will live in your garden year-round, whether in the ground or in containers, and you can nurture them from seedlings and saplings to maturity. Annuals are meant to be replaced every year; they'll grace you with blooms all season long and die off in the winter. (Some perennial plants are grown and treated as annuals in certain harsher climates. Check the plant's tag to see whether it is an annual or perennial in your zone or region. The hardiness zone where you live indicates what plants can thrive in your region based on average low temperatures.)

In this chapter, we'll explore each plant category. At the end is a section devoted to houseplants for the indoor moon garden, but many of the outdoor plants described in the night-blooming and night-fragrant sections also make excellent houseplants. A few of these plants are poisonous and should be kept out of reach of children and pets, so always do your research before bringing a plant home.

TIPS FOR
SHOPPING
FOR PLANTS

Check the bloom times across your assortment of plants to ensure you'll have flowers blooming in spring, summer, fall, and even winter.

Make sure the plants' tags indicate that they're hardy to your growing zone [see the zone map on page 154].

It requires patience, but buying plants in smaller sizes is more economical. To strike a balance, buy mature sizes of slower-growing plants and smaller faster-growing plants.

If your local nursery doesn't have what you're looking for, consider another variety with a similar shape, structure, and bloom time.

Don't buy just one of any variety; buy three, five, or more to plant in groups.

Ask for assistance! Nursery staff are very knowledgeable and know their stock. And who doesn't love talking about plants?

Night-blooming Plants

Night-blooming, or nocturnal, plants
open their flowers in the evening to attract
nocturnal pollinators like moths and
bats. Some open at twilight; others wait
until full darkness. Many night-blooming
species are native to tropical regions
and therefore cannot survive outdoors
in the cold winters of much of North
America. If you live in a cold region, you
can grow these plants in pots outdoors
in the summer and, in some cases, bring
them indoors for the winter, to either a
greenhouse or a full-sun spot in your home.
Some species are best treated as annuals
and can be replaced yearly. The following
plants are noteworthy night-blooming
species for a moon garden.

Brugmansia suaveolens

ANGEL'S TRUMPET

1

Brugmansia

Type:	Evergreen shrub/ small tree
Sun:	Full sun
Zones:	9-11
Height:	6-10 ft [2-3 m]
Width:	3-10 ft [0.9-3 m]
Use:	Annual

Angel's trumpet, a stunning tropical plant in the Nightshade family, is native to South America. *Brugmansia* grows well in containers and is a showstopper on a terrace or in a backyard both day and night. The flowers release their sweet scent in the evening and mysteriously reach their peak bloom during the full moon. They come in many colors (pinks, yellows, white, and cream) and varieties that reach different heights, including shrubs. Keep their soil most, and in places where the temperature drops below 60°F (15°C), bring them indoors and keep in full sun or a greenhouse. NOTE: All parts of this plant are poisonous.

NICOTIANA

Nicotiana is a genus of flowering tobacco plants native to tropical South America and celebrated for its beautiful flowers and fragrance. Two species in particular are stunners for the night garden.

NIGHT SHOOTING STARS

Nicotiana sylvestris

Type: Herbaceous perennial

Sun: Full sun to partial shade

Zones: 10–11

Height: 3–5 ft [0.9–1.5 m]

Width: 1–2 ft [30–60 cm]

Use: Annual

Also known as the tobacco plant, this night bloomer is from the Andean region of Argentina and Bolivia. Its tubular white flowers resemble shooting stars; planted en masse, it looks like a celestial shower. It can be planted in the spring, grows quickly, and blooms all summer long. If growing from seed, start in the early spring and keep the soil moist. It's typically grown as an annual in temperatures that drop below 50°F (10°C). Its fragrance attracts nocturnal pollinators like hawk moths.

JASMINE TOBACCO

Nicotiana alata

Type: Herbaceous perennial

Sun: Full sun to partial shade

Zones: 10–11

Height: 3–5 ft [0.9–1.5 m]

Width: 1–2 ft [30–60 cm]

Use: Annual

Jasmine tobacco opens its flowers in the evening and releases a sweet fragrance late into the night. Humble during the day, its flowers become spectacular after dusk. A perennial in its native habitat, it is typically grown as an annual in colder climates.

2

Oenothera biennis

EVENING PRIMROSE

2

Oenothera biennis

Type:	Biennial
Sun:	Full sun to partial shade
Zones:	4-9
Height:	3-5 ft [0.9-1.5 m]
Width:	2-3 ft [60-90 cm]
Use:	Native garden

Native to eastern North America, evening primrose bears lovely pale yellow cup-shaped flowers that bloom from dusk to morning, early summer to early fall. Their sweet lemon scent draws in night-pollinating moths as well as birds, butterflies, and bees in daylight. It's a biennial, meaning it has a life cycle of two years; in the first year it grows foliage, and in the second year it flowers and then dies. It is easy to grow from seed—in early summer, sow seeds directly where you intend to grow them, or grow in a pot and transplant in the fall. It readily self-seeds for more evening primrose in your garden for years to come.

3

MOONFLOWER

Ipomoea alba

Type:	Tender perennial vine
Sun:	Full to partial sun
Zones:	10-12
Height:	10-15 ft [3-4.5 m]
Width:	3-6 ft [0.9-1.8 m]
Use:	Annual, trellis, arbor

Moonflower is the most famous of night bloomers, a twining vine with stunning trumpet-shaped white flowers that unfurl at twilight, releasing a sweet lemon scent. The flowers close up as the sun rises, but on overcast days stay open longer. Although a tender perennial, moonflower is grown mostly as an annual in colder climates. You can usually find seeds (the packets are often beautifully illustrated, and worth saving in their own right—you could store little notes, poems, or Polaroid photos in them). Moonflowers are quite easy to grow from seed and bloom in late summer. Keep the soil semimoist. They will need a support structure like a trellis to climb up. Plant it in a container or in the ground.

NIGHT-BLOOMING JASMINE

Cestrum nocturnum

Type:	Evergreen shrub
Sun:	Full sun to partial shade
Zones:	9-11
Height:	8-10 ft [2.4-3 m]
Width:	4-6 ft [1.2-1.8 m]
Use:	Annual, containers

This shrub originally from the West Indies is in fact not a true jasmine. While its flowers are tiny, come nightfall their aroma is so strong it will reach your neighbors' yard and may even overpower more sensitive noses. It blooms all summer and attracts hawk moths. NOTE: All parts are toxic to humans and pets, and it's invasive in certain states, so use a planter for root containment.

TUBEROSE

Agave amica (formerly *Polianthes tuberosa*)

Type:	Perennial bulb
Sun:	Full sun
Zones:	7-10
Height:	2-3 ft [60-90 cm]
Width:	2-3 ft [60-90 cm]
Use:	Annual, containers

Loved for its delicious, sensual fragrance, tuberose has been used in perfumes since the seventeenth century. Originally from Mexico, its flowers are commonly used in Hawaiian leis. Blooming in late summer and fall evenings, spikes of white flowers are waxy and tubular. In colder climates, start bulbs in nursery pots indoors and keep them near a warm, sunny window, transplanting them outside once the threat of frost has passed. Position them near a window to relish their sweet fragrance indoors.

3

Ipomoea alba

ZALUZIANSKYA OVATA

4

NIGHT PHLOX

④

Zaluzianskya ovata

Type:	Perennial
Sun:	Full sun
Zones:	9-11
Height:	6-12 in [15-30 cm]
Width:	12 in [30 cm]
Use:	Annual, containers

This is a small but mightily fragrant plant native to South Africa. Throughout the day its wine-colored buds stay shut; come nightfall, they open into dainty pinkish-white cup-shaped flowers with scalloped edges. Moths love the sweet, spicy scent. It's best grown in a pot because it is not especially cold hardy and needs to be either brought indoors in the winter and stored in a cool place or grown as an annual. It flowers throughout the summer; its short, compact growth habit makes it great in the front of a border. Night phlox enjoys full sun and humus-rich, well-draining soil—keep the soil moist while it's flowering but dry in the winter if overwintering indoors.

HEMEROCALLIS CITRINA

CITRON DAYLILY

5

Hemerocallis citrina

Type: Herbaceous perennial

Sun: Full sun to partial shade

Zones: 3-9

Height: 3-4 ft [0.9-1.2 m]

Width: 1.5-2 ft [45-60 cm]

Use: Mixed border, massed

Despite its name, this daylily is actually a night bloomer. Opening at sunset in June and July, the 6 inch (15 cm) yellow flowers have a strong honeysuckle fragrance in the evening and fade the following morning. Plant in groups and remove spent flowers daily. Its green, blade-like leaves offer interest when the plant is not in bloom.

NIGHT-BLOOMING HOUSEPLANTS

The following night-blooming plants can be kept outdoors in the summer and in tropical climates, but they also make wonderful year-round houseplants for an indoor moon garden.

6

QUEEN OF THE NIGHT

Epiphyllum oxypetalum

Type:	Epiphyte
Sun:	Direct light
Zones:	10-11
Height:	6-10 ft [1.8-3 m]
Width:	3 ft [0.9 m]
Use:	Hanging houseplant

The majestic flowers of this tropical orchid cactus captivate: They bloom one night a year and wilt at dawn. The flowers are silky, extravagant, and white, reaching up to 1 foot (30 cm) long. Even when not flowering, this unique plant—a cactus with smooth, flattened leaves, like thick ribbons with scalloped edges—is worthy of any collection. Unlike desert cacti, this epiphyte from the rainforests of Mexico enjoys more regular watering. It's a great houseplant given bright light; if you do keep it outdoors in the summer, be sure to bring it indoors before the temperature drops to 40°F (4.5°C).

MONSTERA DELICIOSA

Type:	Climbing vine
Sun:	Bright indirect light
Zones:	10-11
Height:	6-15 ft [2-4.5 m]
Width:	2-6 ft [0.6-2 m]
Use:	Accent shrub or vine

Also known as the Swiss cheese plant because of the holes, or fenestrations, in its glossy green leaves, the monstera plant, native to Mexico and Central America, is a popular houseplant. Grown outdoors, fragrant white spathes bloom at night. A delicious edible fruit follows; when ripe, it tastes like a blend of mango and pineapple but with the texture of banana. Its interesting growth habit, vining up trees in the wild, means it can be trained at home to climb a stake or moss pole. Without structural support it will grow to be quite wide. Allow soil to dry out slightly between watering.

6

EPIPHYLLUM OXYPETALUM

7

SELENICEREUS UNDATUS

8

SELENICEREUS ANTHONYANUS

SELENICEREUS

There are hundreds of cactuses that bloom at night. Also known as the moon cactus, the *Selenicereus* genus, native to Mexico, Central America, and the Caribbean, has some of the largest and most exquisite night-fragrant flowers. Its other common name, "night-blooming cereus," is applied to many genera of night-blooming cactuses, including *Epiphyllum* and *Peniocereus*.

DRAGON FRUIT   7

Selenicereus undatus

Type: Vine
Sun: Direct light
Zones: 10-11
Height: 10-20 ft [3-6 m] if grown outdoors
Width: 5-10 ft [1.5-3 m] if grown outdoors
Use: Hanging/climbing

The dragon fruit (*Selenicereus undatus*) is famous for its majestic blooms that open for only one night and for its delicious fruit. Its nocturnal white flowers can reach 1 foot (30 cm) long and are pollinated by bats. With its dramatic vining stems, it is great in a hanging planter with good drainage. For it to bear fruit indoors, it needs a support structure, six to eight hours of direct sun, and possibly hand pollination. *Selenicereus grandiflorus* is another stunning option.

RIC-RAC/FISHBONE/ZIG-ZAG CACTUS   8

Selenicereus anthonyanus

Type: Epiphyte
Sun: Bright indirect light
Zones: 10-11
Height: 2 ft [60 cm]
Width: 2 ft [60 cm]
Use: Hanging

An excellent hanging plant, this cactus adds character to a modern living space with its dramatic silhouette. Blooming for only one night each year, its 4 inch (10 cm) silky flowers of magenta and white petals are as fragrant as they are showy. Easy to care for, this cactus thrives in ambient bright light but is sensitive to overwatering. While tropical cacti enjoy more frequent watering than arid cacti, they still don't like wet feet. Good drainage is essential, as is humidity, so mist regularly. *Epiphyllum anguliger* has a striking resemblance to S. anthonyanus and is also an excellent houseplant.

Night-fragrant Plants

Night-fragrant plants exude powerful
scents in the evenings. Their flowers may
open in the daylight but are most fragrant
from dusk until dawn. Many make
excellent year-round houseplants.

AERANGIS BRACHYCARPA

ANGRAECOID ORCHIDS

9

Type: Epiphyte
Sun: Bright indirect light
Zones: 10-11
Height: Up to 3 ft [0.9 m]
Width: Up to 2 ft [0.6 m]
Use: Hanging houseplant

Darwin's star orchid (*Angraecum sesquipedale*) bears exquisite ivory satin flowers that resemble starfish, are heavily fragrant at night, and have long spurs with nectar stored at the very bottom. It has coevolved with only one type of moth—the hawk moth. Other night-fragrant orchids include *Aerangis fastuosa, Aerangis brachycarpa,* and *Brassavola perrinii.* Orchids love humidity and temperatures between 60° and 70°F (15° and 21°C). Good drainage is essential. In the wild, many orchids are epiphytic, meaning they grow out of the cracks and crevices of trees; indoors, grow them in a mix of fir bark and perlite or mounted on a bark slab with sphagnum moss. They love stability—if your orchid is flourishing in a certain spot, try not to move it around too much.

TILLANDSIA CYANEA

10

11

TILLANDSIA USNEOIDES

BROMELIADS

Bromeliads (*Bromeliaceae*) are a family of epiphytic and terrestrial plants with otherworldly shapes and patterns. They live outdoors in warm climates like Florida but also make amazing houseplants for the moon garden because of their striking foliage, long-lasting blooms, and low maintenance needs.

AIR PLANTS ⓾

Tillandsia

Type:	Epiphyte
Sun:	Bright indirect light
Zone:	11
Length:	3-10 in [7.5-25 cm]
Width:	1-6 in [2.5-15 cm]
Use:	Houseplant

Tillandsias, also known as air plants, have a silvery appearance that comes from the fuzzy trichomes that coat their leaves, collecting water and nutrients from moisture in the air. Indoors, if exposed to enough bright light, tillandsias can bloom with beautiful lemon-scented pink and violet flowers that can last from weeks to months. Mount air plants on pieces of driftwood or cork bark (use liquid glue to get them started; they will eventually attach themselves). Hang them on the wall for a sculptural display or from wire on the branches of larger trees. Some flowering species are fragrant both day and night, like *Tillandsia cyanea*, *T. streptocarpa*, and *T. xiphioides*, while others are fragrant only at night, like *T. dodsonii* and *T. duratii*. Be careful not to overwater air plants—submerge them in room-temperature water once a week for several minutes, then let them dry. In rooms with low humidity, mist them weekly.

SPANISH MOSS ⓫

Tillandsia usneoides

Type:	Epiphyte
Sun:	Bright indirect light
Zones:	8-11
Height:	3-20 ft [0.9-6 m]
Width:	1-3 ft [30-90 cm]
Use:	Hanging

Covered in trichomes, the stems of Spanish moss are entirely silver. The long weeping strands have a dreamlike quality that you can bring into your garden. In the evening, small chartreuse flowers, pollinated by moths, produce a sweet fragrance. In warm regions this southeastern US native can hang from trees year round. In colder climates, bring it indoors before the first frost and drape it on larger indoor trees like *Ficus lyrata* with wire.

MOCK ORANGE

Philadelphus coronarius

Type: Deciduous shrub
Sun: Full sun to partial
         shade
Zones: 4-8
Height: 10-12 ft [3-3.6 m]
Width: 10-12 ft [3-3.6 m]
Use: Hedge

Mock orange is most famous for its profuse evening fragrance and named for its beautiful white flowers that smell of orange blossoms. Its fast growth habit means it will grow to be a large shrub fairly quickly and can be used as a hedge. Passersby may stop to smell these potent spring flowers. Mock orange enjoys full sun and can tolerate partial shade, although its blooms will be more prolific with full sun. Provide rich, well-drained soil. Prune spent flowers and thin branches after flowering.

EUROPEAN HONEYSUCKLE

Lonicera periclymenum

Type: Deciduous shrub
Sun: Full sun to partial
         shade
Zones: 5-9
Height: 10-15 ft [3-4.5 m]
Width: 3-6 ft [0.9-1.8 m]
Use: Vine

This summer-blooming European honeysuckle is far more fragrant at night than during the day, attracting moths, bees, and birds to pink and creamy white blooms that age to a pale yellow. While its flowers and foliage prefer full to part sun, its roots should be planted in the shade. Plant this vigorous climber where it can climb up a bigger structure, like a pergola. Keep soil semi-moist and prune back by up to a third after flowering.

SNAKE PLANT

Dracaena trifasciata

Type:	Herbaceous perennial
Sun:	Direct to low light
Zones:	10-12
Height:	2-4 ft [60-120 cm]
Width:	1-2 ft [30-60 cm]
Use:	Houseplant, hedge
Note:	Previously known as *Sansevieria trifasciata*

The snake plant, also known as mother in law's tongue, is a stiff, upright native to tropical western Africa. It is treasured for being the most low-maintenance houseplant. Preferring dry soil (they almost thrive on neglect), snake plants are wonderful for people who travel a lot for work or may forget to water. They enjoy bright light but are also a go-to for homes that receive lower light like garden-level apartments, basements, and offices. Given enough bright light, they may produce flowers that bloom in the afternoon and evening. The pale green and white petals with long, delicate stamens are very fragrant at night. Even without blooming, at night their yellow-edged leaf blades brighten the garden. Snake plants are susceptible to root rot, so water sparingly. Indoors, water approximately every ten to fourteen days, depending on the light level, and avoid letting water sit in the rosettes.

PLUMERIA

Type:	Deciduous tree
Sun:	Full sun
Zones:	10-12
Height:	15-20 ft [4.5-6 m] if grown outdoors
Width:	15-20 ft [4.5-6 m] if grown outdoors
Use:	Small tree, Houseplant

Plumeria, also known as frangipani, produces a lovely fragrance at night to attract sphinx moths to pollinate them. Endemic to Mexico, Central America, and the Caribbean, plumerias have become naturalized in many countries; its delicate flowers are used to make leis in Hawaii and the Pacific Islands. If given at least six hours of full sun and with proper watering, plumeria can be grown as a year-round houseplant. They do not like wet feet and require excellent drainage in containers. If you live in a cooler climate, grow plumeria in a pot outdoors in the summer and bring it indoors before temperatures drop below 50°F (10°C).

12

Hoya carnosa

HOYA CARNOSA 'KRIMSON QUEEN'

12

Type:	Evergreen vine
Sun:	Bright indirect light
Zones:	9-11
Height:	2-4 ft [60-120 cm] Long vines, cascading/climbing plant
Use:	Hanging houseplant

The vast *Hoya* genus (comprising over five hundred species native to Southeast Asia, Oceania, and Australia) offers exquisite flowers in white and shades of pink and yellow. On mature plants, clusters of waxy buds open into tiny star-shaped blooms. *Hoya carnosa* 'Krimson Queen' has tricolor leaves marked white, light pink, and green—perfect for a moon garden. To encourage flowering, give it bright light and less frequent water. Hoyas make excellent hanging plants, cascading or climbing up wire, leather cord, and macramé, giving your indoor garden a lush and wild look.

Perennials, Annuals, and Bulbs

These plants will fill your outdoor planters, garden beds, and window boxes with fragrant, showy flowers. Annuals complete their life cycle in one growing season, so you will plant new ones every year. Perennials are usually cold-hardy plants that go fallow in the winter and come back in the spring, flowering year after year. Some plants in this chapter (noted as such) are tender perennials in warmer climates but treated as annuals in colder climates.

DICENTRA SPECTABILIS

13

BLEEDING HEART

13

Dicentra

Type:	Herbaceous perennial
Sun:	Partial shade
Zones:	3-9
Height:	2-3 ft [60-90 cm]
Width:	1-3 ft [30-90 cm]
Use:	Woodland garden, shaded border, massed

This cottage garden favorite with fern-like foliage bears dainty heart-shaped spring flowers that resemble lockets dangling from thin, arching stalks. At the tip of each heart, protruding inner petals resemble a droplet of blood. They come in shades of pink and white; for the moon garden, try the white varieties *D. spectabilis* 'Alba' and *D. formosa* 'Aurora.' Wonderful in woodland gardens, bleeding hearts pair well with ferns and hostas. Given consistently moist soil, they can tolerate sun.

CHRISTMAS ROSE

Helleborus niger

Type:	Evergreen perennial
Sun:	Partial to full shade
Zones:	3-8
Height:	8-12 in [20-30 cm]
Width:	12-18 in [30-45 cm]
Use:	Woodland garden, ground cover, containers, massed

A must-have in the moon garden, especially in colder climates, hellebores are among the few plants that bloom in late winter. *H. niger*'s large white flowers are especially welcome and vibrant on a cold winter night as they reflect moonlight above a blanket of snow. Plant them in shady front yards and woodland gardens at the base of trees and shrubs in moist, rich soil. It makes an excellent cut flower. NOTE: The leaves and roots are poisonous.

YARROW

Achillea millefolium

Type:	Herbaceous perennial
Sun:	Full sun
Zones:	3-9
Height:	2-3 ft [60-90 cm]
Width:	2-3 ft [60-90 cm]
Use:	Native garden, meadow, containers

This hardy perennial genus won't let you down. Yarrow 'Moonshine' has lemon yellow, flattened flowers on tall stems from June to September, attracting pollinators. The unique floral shape adds a dreamy, ethereal quality to a meadow moon garden, and its yellow flowers and lacy silver-gray foliage glow softly in the moonlight. 'Moon Dust' has ivory-yellow flowers. Grow in a cottage or naturalistic garden, containers, borders, and meadows. They handle dry heat and prefer semidry soil.

CONEFLOWER

Echinacea purpurea

Type:	Herbaceous perennial
Sun:	Full sun
Zones:	3-8
Height:	2-3 ft [60-90 cm]
Width:	1-2 ft [30-60 cm]
Use:	Native garden, meadow, containers

These native perennials are a staple in any style of garden, adding splashes of color, height, and structure all summer long. Ideal for a moon garden, 'White Swan' and 'Pow Wow White' offer large flowers with delicate white petals. Mass several plants or mingle with black-eyed Susans (*Rudbeckia*) and hummingbird mint (*Agastache*). As they go to seed in fall, the conical flower heads turn black, adding drama through winter and attracting birds like goldfinches that feast on their seeds. Their drought tolerance makes them a good choice for rooftops and terraces.

BEE BLOSSOM

Gaura lindheimeri

Type:	Herbaceous perennial
Sun:	Full sun
Zones:	5-9
Height:	15-48 in[38-122 cm]
Width:	15-48 in[38-122 cm]
Use:	Native garden, containers, annual

Also known as 'Whirling Butterflies,' this southern native perennial has striking flowers that "flutter" atop tall, arching stems. With very long-lasting blooms in shades of white and pink, gaura is an ethereal addition to a romantic moon garden. Drought and heat tolerant, it is great in borders, window boxes, and containers. Cut back to the ground in the fall. Scarlet gaura (*G. coccinea*) is a night-blooming option.

FOXGLOVE

14

Digitalis purpurea

Type:	Biennial
Sun:	Partial shade
Zones:	4-8
Height:	3-5 ft [0.9-1.5 m]
Width:	1.5-2 ft [45-60 cm]
Use:	Cottage garden, mixed bed

Foxglove's tall, spring-blooming spires grace woodland or cottage gardens with decadent elegance. The pure white *Digitalis purpurea f. albiflora* will be the star of any moon garden.

NOTE: Foxgloves are poisonous and should be kept away from children and pets.

COSMOS

15

Type:	Annual
Sun:	Full sun
Zones:	2-11
Height:	1-6 ft [30-180 cm]
Width:	1-3 ft [30-90 cm]
Use:	Annual, mixed border

Cosmos are a lovely annual to bring motion and whimsy to your garden. Dainty saucer-shaped flowers swing on thread-like stems above ferny foliage. Cosmos flowers come in a wide color range, including white, yellows, oranges, pinks, reds, and magenta. For the moon garden, try the white *Cosmos bipinnatus* 'Sonata White' (1–2 feet tall, 1–2 feet wide) or *Cosmos sulphureus* 'Cosmic Yellow,' a dwarf golden yellow variety great for containers. Cosmos love sun and bloom summer into fall, thronged with bees and butterflies. Use in annual borders and as cut flowers. Best protected from heavy winds.

14

DIGITALIS PURPUREA

15

COSMOS BIPINNATUS

SPIDER FLOWER

Cleome hassleriana
'White Queen'

Type:	Tender perennial
Sun:	Full sun
Zones:	10-11
Height:	3-4 ft [0.9-1.2 m]
Width:	1-2 ft [30-60 cm]
Use:	Annual, mixed border, containers

Bringing height and glamour to a mixed bed or container arrangement, Cleome is surprisingly heat and drought tolerant. Its striking globe-shaped flowers bob atop tall stems beginning in early summer and continuing through to September.

CHAMOMILE

Type:	Herbaceous perennial
Sun:	Full sun to partial shade
Zones:	2-9
Height:	8-24 in [20-60 cm]
Width:	8-12 in [20-30 cm]
Use:	Annual, herb

Chamomile can be a soothing addition to the moon garden. Roman chamomile is a perennial known for its scent; the flowers and leaves of annual German chamomile are harvested for chamomile tea. Both flower best in full sun. These summer bloomers are most attractive in a container where their adorable daisy-like flowers can shine, with easy access for harvesting. Chamomile has been used to treat sleeplessness, inflammation, and digestive issues. Use the flowers fresh or dried.

SWEET ALYSSUM

Lobularia maritima

Type:	Herbaceous perennial
Sun:	Full to partial sun
Zones:	5-9
Height:	3-10 in [7-25 cm]
Width:	2-4 in [5-10 cm]
Use:	Annual, bedding, containers

This small annual actually prefers colder climates and blooms in cool temperatures, emitting a wonderful honey fragrance. With its trailing, spreading habit, sweet alyssum makes a great border plant in containers and spiller in window boxes. It pairs beautifully with boxwoods. Alyssum self-seeds and is invasive in certain regions.

CLEOME HASSLERIANA

WINDFLOWER / JAPANESE ANEMONE

Anemone x hybrida

Type:	Herbaceous perennial
Sun:	Full sun to partial shade
Zones:	4-8
Height:	2-4 ft [0.6-1.2 m]
Width:	1.5-3 ft [0.5-1 m]
Use:	Woodland garden, cottage garden, mixed border, containers

Commonly known as Japanese anemone but in fact native to China, this seemingly delicate perennial is a hardy late summer and fall bloomer. Cup-shaped flowers sway atop wiry stems with broad, attractive foliage. Pale pink and white hybridized cultivars like 'September Charm' and 'Honorine Jobert' planted in groups will bring style and grace to a moon garden. They are vigorous growers with rhizomatous roots and will spread to any available space: Keep an eye on them or plant them in containers. Anemones thrive in woodland gardens and on sunny rooftops with soil kept evenly moist.

17

DAHLIA 'WHITE ONESTA'

BULBS

Spring-blooming bulbs are best planted in the fall, summer-blooming bulbs in spring. Bulbs are affordable and fun to plant; there's always an element of surprise when they begin sprouting. The term "bulb" also refers to corms, tubers, and rhizomes. Use in border plantings, garden beds, and window boxes.

DAFFODILS

Type:	Bulb
Sun:	Partial shade
Zones:	4-8 [in higher zones the bulbs may need a chilling period]
Height:	6 in-2.5 ft [15-76 cm]
Width:	6-12 in [15-30 cm]
Use:	Annual

Daffodils bring us a joyful spring welcome. They come in many varieties and look great planted en masse, whether a single type or a mixture. Try them as a border along a path or in your front yard. They can be accompanied by other bulbs such as crocuses, snowdrops, and tulips, or by daylilies, which will bloom in early summer after the daffodils. One popular species, *Narcissus tazetta*, bears flower clusters with lemon yellow centers and soft white petals; there are many named cultivars. Also in the *Narcissus* genus, jonquils have been favorites in historic moon gardens for their fragrance. *N. jonquilla* 'Silver Smiles' has ivory petals and buttery yellow cups. Indoors, paperwhites (*Narcissus papyraceus*) are a cheery addition for heavily fragrant winter blooms. (See How to Force Paperwhites Indoors on page 58.)

DAHLIAS

Type:	Tuber
Sun:	Full sun to partial sun
Zones:	8-10
Height:	1-8 ft [30 cm-2.4 m]
Width:	1-2 ft [30-60 cm]
Use:	Annual

Dahlias (grown from tubers, not bulbs) bring a showy elegance to the night garden; their gorgeous rounded flower heads bloom from midsummer well into fall. There are many white-flowered varieties to choose from; look for the waterlily form (resembling tropical water lilies), 'Small World' (pompon flowers that look like little moons), and 'Fleurel' with gigantic yet delicate blooms. Dahlias look best when planted in groups and work well in perennial borders and container gardens. They thrive in rich, well-draining soil.

CALADIUM 'MOONLIGHT'   ⬤18

Type:	Tuber
Sun:	Partial to full shade
Zones:	9-11
Height:	1-3 ft [30-90 cm]
Width:	1-3 ft [30-90 cm]
Use:	Annual

Caladiums are tropical bulb-grown plants with large heart-shaped leaves that come in a dazzling array of colors and patterns. They require part shade and grow well in containers as centerpieces in arrangements and also grouped in a border with other caladium varieties. For the moon garden, try caladium 'Moonlight' with its white and pale green foliage. They thrive in a humid environment with evenly moist soil. They can be kept indoors but are happiest and easier to care for outdoors.

ALLIUM   ⬤19

Type:	Bulb
Sun:	Full sun
Zones:	4-8
Height:	2-4 ft [60-120 cm]
Width:	0.5-1.5 ft [15-45 cm]
Use:	Annual

Alliums bring an easy air of sophistication and structure to a garden. The tall stems topped with globe-shaped flowers are distinctive and architectural, as well as pollinator friendly. Members of the onion family, they come in many colors, sizes, and varieties. For the evening garden, try *Allium stipitatum* 'Mount Everest,' with impressive 6 inch (15 cm) flower heads on stems 2 to 3 feet (60 to 90 cm) tall, or the even taller 'White Giant.' Alliums love full sun, blooming in late spring and early summer. Plant the bulbs in the fall toward the back of a garden border. Deer generally avoid them. *Allium christophii* is notable for its star-shaped flowers forming huge celestial spheres.

CALADIUM 'MOONLIGHT'

18

ALLIUM CHRISTOPHII 19

Silver Foliage

Plants with silver foliage work wonders in
the moon garden palette, adding shimmer,
texture, and contrast to green foliage and
flowering plants. They tend to thrive in full
sun and hot, dry conditions, making them
ideal candidates for spots in the garden
where other plant varieties may struggle.

20

LAVANDULA ANGUSTIFOLIA

LAVENDER

20

Lavandula angustifolia 'Hidcote'

Type:	Herbaceous perennial
Sun:	Full sun
Zones:	5-8
Height:	1-1.5 ft [30-45 cm]
Width:	1-1.5 ft [30-45 cm]
Use:	Hedge, herb, mixed bed, containers

Loved for its fragrance and soothing properties, lavender is a must-have in a sunny moon garden. With silver-gray mounded foliage, lavender makes an elegant hedge plant bordering paths, and is also well suited to growing in planters, thriving in hot, dry conditions like terraces and rooftops.

Lavender 'Ghostly Princess' is a pretty variety with icy silver-gray leaves and violet flowers. In folk medicine, pillows were filled with lavender flowers to calm restlessness and aid sleep. Its essential oil is used medicinally to treat insomnia, anxiety, and hair loss.

ARTEMISIA

The genus Artemisia contains over two hundred species of shrubs and perennials, many with silver-toned foliage; the following are perfect for the evening garden. They prefer dry growing conditions and are drought tolerant.

ARTEMISIA SCHMIDTIANA 'SILVER MOUND'

Type: Semi-evergreen perennial
Sun: Full sun
Zones: 3-7
Height: 8-10 in [20-25 cm]
Width: 10-24 in [25-60 cm]
Use: Ground cover, border, rock garden

Artemisia schmidtiana, native to Japan, has a compact, mounded shape that resembles a fluffy cushion. Planted en masse, it can mirror an expanse of billowing clouds. The lacy foliage is aromatic and silky soft. It grows well in full sun and hot, dry conditions; try it as a ground cover in edging or in a rock garden. 'Silver Mound' also grows well in containers. It can be divided every few years; if it begins to lose shape and density in the center, cut back after it blooms in late summer.

ARTEMISIA ARBORESCENS 'POWIS CASTLE'

Type: Herbaceous perennial
Sun: Full sun
Zones: 3-9
Height: 3 ft [90 cm]
Width: 2 ft [60 cm]
Use: Ground cover, border, rock garden

'Powis Castle' is a bushy artemisia that grows much larger than 'Silver Mound' but with a similar mounding growth habit. Its finely textured leaves are also fragrant and soft. The flowers are inconspicuous. It enjoys full sun and complements showier flowering perennials and ornamental grasses.

LAMB'S EARS

Stachys byzantina

Type:	Herbaceous perennial
Sun:	Full to partial sun
Zones:	4-8
Height:	9-18 in [23-45 cm]
Width:	12-18 in [30-45 cm]
Use:	Ground cover, border, rock garden

Lamb's ears' soft, velvety leaves really do resemble a lamb's ears and are soothing to the touch. It is a hardy, go-to ground cover that can handle full sun and part shade. While its leaves are the main attraction for a night garden, its spires of late spring flowers are also attractive. It grows well both in containers and around the base of specimen trees and shrubs.

WHITE SAGE

Salvia apiana

Type:	Evergreen perennial shrub
Sun:	Full to partial sun
Zones:	8-11
Height:	3-5 ft [0.9-1.5 m]
Width:	3-8 ft [0.9-2.4 m]
Use:	Native garden, herb

Also known as sacred sage, this perennial is native to the southwestern United States and northwestern Mexico. The white-tinged light gray leaves produce a strong aroma when rubbed together. Indigenous peoples of North America have long used white sage in spiritual rituals to cleanse the mind, body, and home. To grow white sage in your garden, keep the soil on the dry side; as a desert plant, it requires little water. You can also expect visits from pollinators like bumblebees and hummingbirds.

ANGEL WINGS

Senecio candicans

Type:	Tender perennial
Sun:	Full to partial sun
Zones:	8-11
Height:	10-16 in [25-40 cm]
Width:	10-16 in [25-40 cm]
Use:	Annual

This member of the dusty miller family has stunning broad leaves with a striking silver sheen that is incredibly soft to the touch. It is excellent in a container and as a showy border plant. Keep the soil evenly moist.

21   *JACOBAEA MARITIMA*

22

DICHONDRA ARGENTEA

SILVER RAGWORT

21

Jacobaea maritima

Type: Tender perennial
Sun: Full sun to partial shade
Zones: 8-11
Height: 6-24 in [15-60 cm]
Width: 6-12 in [15-30 cm]
Use: Annual

Silver ragwort, better known as dusty miller, is a tender perennial from the Mediterranean. The fine hairs, or tomentum, on its leaves and stems give it a felted, woolly texture and bright silvery sheen. One of the most striking plants for a moon garden, it is best used as a border in planters, window boxes, and garden beds. And interestingly, some species of bees use this tomentum, or woolly surface, to build nests.

SILVER NICKEL VINE

22

Dichondra argentea

Type: Herbaceous perennial
Sun: Full to partial sun
Zones: 10-12
Height: 3 in [9 cm]
Width: 3-4 ft [0.9-1.2 m]
Use: Annual

This delicate silver annual works beautifully trailing out of window boxes and containers and as a ground cover at the base of trees. *Dichondra argentea* is native to the desert regions of the southwestern United States and northern Mexico.

Climbing Vines

In addition to the night-blooming and night-fragrant vines described earlier in this chapter (such as moonflower and honeysuckle), the following vines will transform any ordinary fence or wall into a stunning accent wall and lush background. Dense, fragrant blooms climbing the walls of the moon garden create an otherworldly feeling. Many of these vines require a support structure to climb, like trellises, arbors, and pergolas. These can be made of various materials (wood, steel, wire) and take many shapes (arched, leaves, even moon shapes!).

23

JASMINUM POLYANTHUM

PINK JASMINE

23

Jasminum polyanthum

Type:	Semi-evergreen twining vine
Sun:	Full sun to partial shade
Zones:	8-11
Height:	Can climb to 20 ft [6 m]
Width:	20 ft [6 m]
Use:	Arbor, fence, houseplant

Elegant, twining vines bear copious pink buds opening into white star-shaped flowers, usually in January, and releasing a heavenly perfume. Climbing and draping over fences and structures, this vine is native to southwestern China and cannot tolerate freezing temperatures. In a colder climate, you can grow it in a pot outdoors in the summer, bring it indoors before the first frost, and keep it as a houseplant through the winter. Give it a sunny, humid spot where you can enjoy the fragrance from the late winter blooms for several weeks.

STAR JASMINE

Trachelospermum jasminoides

Type: Semi-evergreen twining vine
Sun: Full sun to partial shade
Zones: 8-10
Height: 3-6 ft [0.9-1.8 m]
Width: 3-6 ft [0.9-1.8 m]
Use: Annual, trellis, containers

In late spring, tiny, creamy white star-shaped blooms smother this plant's glossy dark green foliage. A vigorous grower, the star jasmine requires a trellis to climb, and it benefits from a little training when first starting out (plant ties or binding wire will do). This extremely fragrant plant grows well in planters. If you live in a colder climate, grow as an annual or bring indoors in the winter. Keep the soil slightly moist and well drained. Prune after flowering.

CLIMBING HYDRANGEA

Hydrangea petiolaris

Type: Deciduous climbing vine
Sun: Full sun to full shade
Zones: 4-9
Height: 30-50 ft [9-15 m]
Width: 4-6 ft [1.2-1.8 m]
Use: Wall, fence

Blooming in early summer, this stunning climber is grown for its flowers but also has attractive foliage. It's a win-win plant: it needs no trellis to climb and tolerates a variety of light conditions, from full sun to full shade (although if grown in full sun, it does prefer some afternoon shade). This beauty does require patience—it illustrates the saying "First year sleep, second year creep, third year leap." It blooms on old wood, so prune only immediately after blooming ends.

VIRGINIA CREEPER

Parthenocissus quinquefolia

Type: Deciduous climbing vine
Sun: Full sun to partial shade
Zones: 3-8
Height: 30-50 ft [9-15 m]
Width: 5-10 ft [1.5-3 m]
Use: Wall, ground cover, native garden

A personal favorite, this vine is hardy and reliable. Loved for its foliage, Virginia creeper will quickly creep up walls and fences with its sticky tendrils—no need for a trellis. In autumn, the leaves turn a brilliant red. This vine is superior to ivy because it is native to North America, pollinator friendly, and does not harm trees that it climbs up.

24

CLEMATIS MONTANA

24

CLEMATIS

Clematis montana

Type:	Deciduous twining vine
Sun:	Full sun to partial shade
Zones:	6-9
Height:	20-40 ft [6-12 m]
Width:	8-15 ft [2.4-4.5 m
Use:	Arbor, fence

Several varieties of clematis make beautiful vines, with different cultivars blooming at different times of the year. *Clematis montana*, a vigorous climber, blooms in late spring, revealing hundreds of white 3 to 4 inch (7.5 to 10 cm) fragrant flowers with yellow stamens. It's also called anemone clematis for its resemblance to anemone flowers. Plant with roots in shade and keep the soil moist but not soggy. Newly planted vines benefit from a little training up the trellis. Clematis pairs beautifully with climbing roses.

PASSIONFLOWER

25

Passiflora incarnata

Type:	Evergreen twining vine
Sun:	Full sun to partial shade
Zones:	5-9
Height:	6-8 ft [1.8-2.4 m]
Width:	3-6 ft [0.9-1.8 m]
Use:	Trellis, fence, native garden

Blooming from midsummer to early fall, this gorgeous flowering vine looks tropical but is in fact native to the southeastern United States. The striking flowers, with fringe-like petals in concentric rings of purple and white, attract butterflies.

Rounded edible fruits called maypops can be eaten fresh and also make a popular jelly. While vigorous, this climber prefers the shelter of a wall. It is drought tolerant and prefers a well-draining soil.

TRUMPET HONEYSUCKLE

26

Lonicera sempervirens

Type:	Deciduous twining vine
Sun:	Full sun
Zones:	4-9
Height:	8-15 ft [2.4-4.5 m]
Width:	3-6 ft [0.9-1.8 m]
Use:	Trellis, fence, native garden

This beloved honeysuckle comes in a variety of colors (coral, red, and gold); for the moon garden, try *Lonicera sempervirens* 'John Clayton,' with lightly fragrant, buttery yellow flowers. Native to eastern North America, this plant is a hummingbird favorite. Honeysuckle needs a structure to climb; one option is to plant it in the ground or a large pot at the base of an outdoor staircase and train it to climb up the handrail.

CLIMBING ROSE

Type:	Deciduous shrub
Sun:	Full sun to partial shade
Zones:	5-9
Height:	8-12 ft [2.4-3.6 m]
Width:	3-6 ft [0.9-1.8 m]
Use:	Arbor, trellis, containers

Roses are classic and timeless. To create a romantic, secret garden vibe, plant climbing roses. Not technically a vine, climbing roses need attaching and training to a support structure like a trellis to climb up and are stunning when clambering up arbors or draping over gazebos with their dense, prolific blooms. Grow on an arch to welcome you into your garden. 'Rosa Clarence House' is a reliable choice that will brighten a night garden with blooms from June to September. Most roses need full sun to bloom, so locate them accordingly. They do welcome a bit of afternoon shade. Roses grow well both in containers and in the ground.

25

PASSIFLORA INCARNATA

26

LONICERA SEMPERVIRENS

Shrubs and Trees

Woody shrubs and trees bring form and
structure to the garden. Whether deciduous
or evergreen, they can act as stunning
specimens, stealing the nightly show,
or can be planted in groups to provide
background interest for other flowering
plants. Often, a mix of both is in order.

HYDRANGEA

Gardeners can rely on hydrangeas to bloom in the heat of midsummer—a time when many other shrubs are not flowering—and well into the fall, with inflorescence fading to a deep rosy pink and foliage turning burgundy. Dried flower heads offer winter beauty.

OAK-LEAF HYDRANGEA

Hydrangea quercifolia

Type: Deciduous shrub
Sun: Full sun to partial shade
Zones: 5-9
Height: 4-6 ft [1.2-1.8 m]
Width: 4-6 ft [1.2-1.8 m]
Use: Accent, hedge, mixed shrub border

This woody flowering shrub, native to the southeastern United States, is a reliable favorite in East Coast gardens. Low maintenance, it also offers structure and volume in the garden. Showy panicles of flowers up to 8 inches (20 cm) long bloom for months with a subtly sweet scent, beginning in early to midsummer. The dark green oak-leaf-shaped foliage is a lovely contrast to the lighter green leaves of other hydrangea varieties. Keep the soil semi-moist.

PANICLE HYDRANGEA

Hydrangea paniculata

Type: Deciduous shrub
Sun: Full sun to partial shade
Zones: 3-8
Height: 6-8 ft [1.8-2.5 m]
Width: 6-8 ft [1.8-2.5 m]
Use: Accent, hedge, mixed shrub border

Native to China and Japan, this hardy hydrangea boasts impressive creamy white flowers. The cultivar 'Quick fire' possesses pale pink and white flowers, while 'Limelight' has panicles tinged lime green. This large, upright shrub makes both an excellent hedge and statement plant, and needs rich, semi-moist, well-draining soil. Flower buds form on current season's growth, so prune in late winter or early spring. For smaller gardens or containers, try 'Little Lime' hydrangea (3–5 ft [1–1.5 m] tall and wide).

27

VIBURNUM PLICATUM

VIBURNUM

Viburnum, a genus of prolific shrubs with dense foliage and beautiful spring blooms, is a wonderful option for shadier moon gardens.

KOREAN SPICE VIBURNUM

Viburnum carlesii

Type: Deciduous shrub
Sun: Full sun to partial shade
Zones: 4-7
Height: 4-6 ft [1.2-1.8 m]
Width: 4-7 ft [1.2-2.1 m]
Use: Mixed shrub border

Named for its strong yet buoyant sweet fragrance, this compact shrub forms clusters of glossy blush pink buds that open into tiny star-shaped white flowers in spring. Consider planting a viburnum near your bedroom window so that its sweet scent wafts in as you fall asleep. Grow in semi-moist, well-drained soil and prune after flowering. A larger option with exquisite fragrance is the hybrid *Viburnum* x *carlcephalum*.

JAPANESE SNOWBALL

27

Viburnum plicatum

Type: Deciduous shrub
Sun: Full sun to partial shade
Zones: 5-8
Height: 8-15 ft [2.4-4.5 m]
Width: 10-18 ft [3-5 m]
Use: Specimen, mixed shrub border

This viburnum's bright white, perfectly rounded blooms have earned it the name Japanese snowball. Non-fragrant flowers open in mid-spring and leaves turn burgundy red in fall. F. *plicatum* is the cultivated sterile species that does not bear fruit; it is actually derived from the wild species f. *tomentosum* that grows native in the forests of Japan and China. This dense, extravagant shrub can stand on its own or be planted in a bed with other contrasting shrubs. Prune after flowering.

MAGNOLIA

The *Magnolia* genus is prehistoric—fossils date magnolias back ninety million years. They came into existence before bees and are in fact pollinated by beetles. Many magnolia flowers, or tepals, open at night and are extremely night-fragrant.

SWEETBAY MAGNOLIA

Magnolia virginiana

Type:	Semi-evergreen tree
Sun:	Full sun to partial shade
Zones:	5-10
Height:	10-35 ft [2.5-10.7 m]
Width:	10-35 ft [2.5-10.7 m]
Use:	Specimen tree, multi-stemmed shrub

The elegant sweetbay magnolia is native to the US East Coast from Atlanta to New York. Spring flowers are cup shaped, creamy white, and sweetly lemon scented, especially at night. It is best suited to a large garden. The foliage is evergreen in the South. Keep the soil evenly moist; this magnolia variety can handle boggier conditions.

SOUTHERN MAGNOLIA

Magnolia grandiflora

Type:	Broadleaf evergreen tree
Sun:	Full sun to partial shade
Zones:	7-9
Height:	60-80 ft [18.2-24.4 m]
Width:	30-50 ft [9-15 m]
Use:	Specimen

Southern magnolia is a stately evergreen tree native to the southeastern United States. Its glossy dark green leaves with copper-toned undersides contrast beautifully with its gorgeous ivory flowers, blooming throughout the summer. In ideal conditions, it can reach 80 feet (24.4 m) tall, so it is not for small spaces. Grow in organically rich, moist, well-drained soil.

28

CORNUS FLORIDA

FLOWERING DOGWOOD

28

Cornus florida

Type:	Deciduous tree
Sun:	Full sun to partial shade
Zones:	5-9
Height:	15-30 ft [4.5-9 m]
Width:	15-30 ft [4.5-9 m]
Use:	Specimen, native and woodland garden

This dogwood's growth structure feels hopeful: Its branches stretch outward and upward, with spring flowers opening to the sun as if floating on their backs. With its branches covered in blooms, it creates a gorgeous canopy that shines brightly in the moonlight. The white variety possesses brilliant flowers with a slight yellow tint. Good for smaller gardens, they enjoy dappled shade and can do well in a north-facing yard, although their blooms will be even more prolific in full sun. Give them moist (but never soggy) acidic soil. *Cornus kousa,* a pink-flowering native of China, Korea, and Japan, is another beautiful option.

29

CITRUS TREE

29

CITRUS TREE

Type:	Broadleaf evergreen shrub/tree
Sun:	Full sun
Zones:	11
Height:	6 ft [1.8 m]
Width:	3 ft [0.9 m]
Use:	Indoor/outdoor

Few garden endeavors are as delightful as growing your own fruit tree. A lemon or lime tree or shrub in a planter can flourish outdoors in the summer and move indoors before the first frost; give it a full sun spot near a window, and keep it in cooler temperatures in order to produce fruit and flower during its winter dormancy period. Citrus plants need humidity and good air circulation. Keep the soil moist but not soggy.

WEEPING CHERRY

Prunus 'Snow Fountain'

Type: Deciduous tree
Sun: Full sun to partial shade
Zones: 5-8
Height: 15-25 ft [4.5-7.6 m]
Width: 15-25 ft [4.5-7.6 m]
Use: Specimen

Japanese cherry trees are celebrated for their magnificent spring blossoms. Several cultivars can star in a moon garden. For a romantic look in a smaller yard, try the compact weeping cherry 'Snow Fountain.' In bloom, its downward cascading branches resemble a fountain of white blossoms: instant curb appeal. Allow a sphere of space around the trunk base so the branches can "weep" gracefully without obstructions. Beyond this sphere, choose shorter plants so as not to visually compete with the elegance of the tree—try a silvery ground cover like lamb's ears on page 107. Cherries need well-draining soil.

SERVICEBERRY

Amelanchier canadensis

Type: Deciduous shrub/ tree
Sun: Full sun to partial shade
Zones: 4-8
Height: 15-30 ft [4.5-9 m]
Width: 15-20 ft [4.5-6 m]
Use: Mixed shrub border, specimen, native garden

This large shrub or small tree is a jewel in any garden, with showy white flowers in early spring and edible berries in early summer (try serviceberry pie!). Come fall, its leaves turn a vibrant red. Native to eastern North America, it is attractive to both birds and humans. It can thrive in a planter or woodland garden. Container plants will not reach full size. Berries from the Saskatoon Serviceberry (*Amelanchier alnifolia*) also make a delicious pie.

PAPER BIRCH

Betula papyrifera

Type: Tree
Sun: Partial shade
Zones: 2-6
Height: 50-75 ft [15-23 m]
Width: 25-50 ft [7.6-15 m]
Use: Grove of trees

The delicate texture and silvery white tones of the paper birch tree's bark stand out in the darkness, adding a mystical vibe to the moon garden. It's a fine specimen tree, but if you have the space, these really shine when several are planted together.

SWEET AZALEA

Rhododendron arborescens

Type: Deciduous shrub
Sun: Partial shade
Zones: 4-7
Height: 8-20 ft [2.4-6 m]
Width: 8-20 ft [2.4-6 m]
Use: Hedge, mixed shrub
         border

Sweet azalea is named for the flowers' sweet scent, which persists well into the evening. Native to the eastern United States, it blooms in late spring and early summer, attracting hummingbirds and butterflies. Give it well-draining acidic soil—it will not do well in clay soil—and protect from strong wind. Prune spent flowers immediately after blooming.

YEW

Taxus baccata

Type: Evergreen shrub
Sun: Full sun to full
         shade
Zones: 6-7
Height: 3-60 ft
         [0.9-18 m],
         depending
         on cultivar
Width: 15-20 ft [4.5-6 m]
Use: Hedge

The Taxus genus comprises coniferous evergreen shrubs and trees that make excellent hedge plants. While slower-growing, this European yew is excellent for shady gardens. In folklore across cultures, the yew is considered sacred. Yews do not like extreme temperatures or wet feet but are very tolerant of pruning. Use as a green backdrop for showy white flowers and silver foliage. Some varieties make an excellent ground cover. All parts of this plant are poisonous.

GARDENIA

Gardenia jasminoides

Type: Broadleaf tender
         evergreen shrub
Sun: Partial shade
Zones: 8-11
Height: 5-6 ft [1.5-1.8 m]
Width: 5-6 ft [1.5-1.8 m]
Use: Indoor/outdoor,
         containers

Gardenias are adored for their large rosette-shaped blooms and deliciously sweet scent. Grow them outdoors in the summer with protection from afternoon sun. Before the first frost, bring them indoors to a covered porch with cooler temperatures where they can lay dormant for the winter. They will bloom profusely in spring. Gardenias enjoy humidity and require well-draining, acidic soil. Water regularly to keep their soil moist. Prune after flowering. Gardenias are susceptible to a variety of pests.

Buxus SEMPERVIRENS

30

BOXWOOD

Buxus sempervirens

Type:	Broadleaf evergreen shrub
Sun:	Full sun to partial shade
Zones:	5-8
Height:	5-15 ft [1.5-4.5 m]
Width:	5-15 ft [1.5-4.5 m]
Habit:	Shrub
Use:	Hedge, containers

Boxwood is an evergreen staple for any moon garden. Vita Sackville-West relied heavily on boxwood to create a green backdrop for her White Garden. In formal gardens boxwood are often shaped into rounded balls, topiaries, and hedges; in mass planting they can offer an undulating, sculptural form. Boxwood needs protection from strong winds and direct winter sun. Accent a garden with boxwoods, ferns, and moss with white anemones, and bleeding hearts. Native alternatives that resemble boxwood are *Ilex glabra* on the East Coast, and Oregon boxwood (*Paxistima myrsinite*s) on the West Coast.

Houseplants

In addition to the night-blooming
cacti, orchids, bromeliads, hoyas, and
dracaenas detailed earlier in this chapter,
the following plants are wonderful
houseplants for some brilliant blooms
and night shimmer in your home. Tip:
Always check the top 2 inches (5 cm) of
soil before watering your houseplants. If
the soil is dry, you can water. If it's moist,
wait and check again in a day or two. Most
houseplants like to be watered every 7 to
10 days.

31

PHALAENOPSIS AMABILIS

MOTH ORCHIDS

31

Phalaenopsis

Type:	Arching epiphyte
Sun:	Bright indirect light
Height:	8-20 in [20-51 cm]
Use:	Flowering plant

Moth orchids are a popular orchid genus. They have no scent, but their stalks of beautiful butterfly-winged flowers produce succeeding blooms from three to nine months, making them stars of an indoor moon garden. They can winter in a south-facing window but in summer need bright indirect light. Orchids prefer to dry out between waterings, then have their rooting medium thoroughly soaked, mimicking rainfall in their native habitat. Give them plenty of air circulation and a well-drained plastic or clay pot filled with bark-based orchid mix. Cut the stalk with spent blooms a half inch (1 cm) above the last dormant node, then patiently await next year's flowering.

SNAKE PLANT

Dracaena Trifasciata 'Sayuri' and 'Bantel's Sensation'

Type: Upright perennial
Sun: Bright indirect light; tolerates low light
Height: 2–3 ft [60–90 cm]
Width: 2–3 ft [60–90 cm]
Use: Hedge, massed

The 'Sayuri' cultivar is an elegant snake plant with pale silvery gray-green leaves and a more relaxed growth habit than its cousins. Like other snake plant varieties, it is low maintenance and low light tolerant but does enjoy filtered bright light and will grow more quickly with more light.

Dracaena trifasciata 'Bantel's Sensation' has white and green leaves with a vertical growth structure. Variegation is best with ambient bright light. *Dracaena trifasciata* 'Moonshine' has broad, pale green leaves. Water when the soil is thoroughly dry.

32

AGLAONEMA 'SILVER BAY'

Aglaonema commutatum

Type: Bushy perennial
Sun: Bright indirect light; tolerates low light
Height: 1–2 ft [30–60 cm]
Width: 1–2 ft [30–60 cm]
Use: Silver foliage

The beautiful broad leaves on this low-maintenance houseplant are bathed in silver. They are shorter, bushier plants with dense foliage and bloom white flowers regularly. While aglaonemas enjoy bright indirect light, they can also grow well in lower-light spaces and add pops of silver foliage to more neglected spaces, like the interior of a bedroom or deep in a living room, further away from the windows. They ask only for water and a good misting every seven to ten days. Wipe down the leaves to keep them free of dust and pests. Aglaonemas are forgiving plants—they handle inconsistent watering and can go a long time without potting up. Just avoid overwatering, and watch for mealybugs. 'Mystic Marble' is another notable variety.

33

POTHOS 'SNOW QUEEN'

Epipremnum aureum

Type: Vine
Sun: Indirect light
Length: 6–10 ft [1.8–3 m]
Use: Hanging

This slightly less common pothos variety is low maintenance like its family members but needs more sunlight. Its white and green marbled leaves cascade beautifully from a hanging planter and add soothing, soft tones to an interior night garden. Keep out of direct sunlight, potted in well-draining soil, and water about once a week. Droopy or curling leaves indicate it needs water.

SCINDAPSUS

Type: Vine
Sun: Bright indirect light; tolerates low light
Length: 1.5-5 ft [0.4-4.5 m]
Width: 1.5-3 ft [45-90 cm]
Use: Hanging, silver foliage

Scindapsus pictus 'Exotica' is essential to any indoor moon garden. Originally from Southeast Asia, it has a trailing growth habit that works wonderfully in a hanging planter or cascading gracefully off of a high shelf to showcase its variegated silver-toned leaves. You can train the vines to crawl along a wall with clear hooks or around window trim—once it gets going, and with proper repotting, its growth seems limitless. It prefers indirect sunlight and can tolerate lower-light conditions, making it a versatile and reliable houseplant when styling interiors and for city living. It is not cold tolerant. Allow to dry out in between waterings; it does not tolerate wet feet. Water every seven to ten days or when the top 2 inches (5 cm) of soil feels dry.

Scindapsus treubii 'Moonlight,' also known as the moonlight scindapsus, is a striking relative. Its pointed leaves look as if they have been hand painted silver with a thick brush. Drape this plant elegantly across a mantel or hang it near the window to catch the moonlight and showcase its luscious, shimmery foliage. They enjoy bright indirect light and prefer to dry out slightly between waterings.

STROMANTHE 'TRIOSTAR'

Stromanthe sanguinea

Type: Bushy perennial
Sun: Bright indirect light
Height: 2-3 ft [60-90 cm]
Width: 2-3 ft [60-90 cm]
Use: Showy foliage

Stromanthe 'Triostar' has bold variegated leaves of forest green and creamy pink, with fuchsia undersides. Place it on a north- or east-facing windowsill or on a tabletop or console to enjoy its foliage from above. In spots where light can pass through the leaves, they will softly radiate pink. Water when the soil begins to dry out.

AGLAONEMA COMMUTATUM

32

33

EPIPREMNUM AUREUM

34

SCINDAPSUS PICTUS

WATERMELON PEPEROMIA

Peperomia argyreia

Type: Compact, small
         perennial
Sun: Bright indirect
         light
Height: 12 in [30 cm]
Width: 8 in [20 cm]
Use: Hanging, silver
         foliage

The watermelon peperomia is definitely crush worthy. Its thick, coin-shaped silver and green leaves resemble the patterned rind of a watermelon. To appreciate their shimmer when light hits them, hang it in a planter in filtered bright light, or place on a shelf or tabletop to show off its foliage. Much like having a human crush, it can sometimes be hard to tell if this plant likes you back, because it's a little fussy. Good drainage is essential. It is susceptible to common pests—wipe down both sides of the leaves weekly to keep them clean. It is sensitive to overwatering: Be mindful to water only when the top 1 to 2 inches (2.5 to 5 cm) of soil feels dry. Fertilize in the spring and summer.

FLAMINGO FLOWER

Anthurium

Type: Compact perennial
Sun: Bright indirect
         light
Height: 1–2 ft [30–60 cm]
Width: 1–2 ft [30–60 cm]
Use: Flowering plant

A seemingly endless profusion of waxy blooms (spathes) unfurl amidst large, heart-shaped leaves. Coming in hues of white, pink, and red, this epiphytic tropical beauty thrives in bright but indirect light to avoid leaf scorch. Water about once a week when the top inch of soil is dry.

KALANCHOE 'AURORA BOREALIS'

Kalanchoe fedtschenkoi variegata

Type: Compact succulent
Sun: Direct light
Height: 1 ft [30 cm]
Width: 1 ft [30 cm]
Use: Dry garden

Make this the centerpiece of a succulent moon garden. Its thick, oval, bluish-green leaves have variegated streaks of cream. When exposed to direct sunlight, the scalloped edges take on a magenta or lavender hue as if outlined in marker. In spring, clusters of dark pink, bell-shaped flowers hang above upright stems.

35

PEPEROMIA ARGYREIA

ENJOYING YOUR MOON GARDEN

Your moon garden can be a site of healing, relaxation, contemplation, and celebration. It's an oasis where you can take time for yourself and revel in nature in a sanctuary of blooming plants. Being in the garden, tending to plants, and watching them grow can be a soulful and spiritual experience. Nurturing your plants also nurtures you.

In this chapter are rituals for deepening your connection with the moon, its phases, and yourself. There are prompts that reconnect you with the marvels of nature and encourage mindful meditation. And you'll find tips for transforming your moon garden into a social space, to share in the wonders of the moon with friends and family.

Entertaining

In Chinese culture, the Moon Festival, or the Mid-Autumn Festival as it's also known, is a traditional annual holiday that celebrates the autumn's harvest and its massive, golden moon. Each year my family celebrates the festival by eating moon cakes, watching the huge harvest moon rise, lighting lanterns, and reciting Chinese classical poems to the moon. As children we'd also look for the rabbit—in East Asian folklore, the rabbit lives on the moon with a mortar and pestle, pounding herbs to make immortality potions for the gods.

The harvest moon is especially dramatic and invites an occasion. But no matter the lunar phase, your moon garden can be a perfect place to gather. Depending on your garden's size, plan a romantic candlelit dinner for two among the foliage, or a festive dinner party under the stars. Here are a few more ideas to inspire your own moon garden parties.

HOST A FULL MOON PARTY

Celebrate the full moon with a feast and friends. It'll be extra luminous if your party falls on a supermoon!

Host a potluck or prepare a multicourse meal, ideally featuring local seasonal ingredients. When possible, shop at your local farmers' market so you can meet the farmers who grew the food you'll enjoy.

The tone of your party will be set by the ambience you create and the company you keep, and this includes the moon itself! Invite friends who inspire you, encourage growth, and illuminate your life.

Whether your party is indoors or outdoors, make some lustrous floral arrangements and dot them around your space. Think bouquets of voluminous, light-colored, moon-shaped flowers like white hydrangeas, or fragrant flowers like peonies or lilies—whatever is in bloom and excites you.

On the night of the full moon, a celestial mysteriousness and celebratory aura fill the air. Ask your guests to wear white or light tones or something shimmery that will softly glow in the moonlight. Invite them to arrive in time for everyone to await the moonrise together.

Light citronella candles, lanterns, and tea lights. If you choose to play music, keep it low so people can hear the sounds of the birds and the natural world. Give your guests a tour of the garden and invite them to delight in the most fragrant flowers.

GATHER FOR A NIGHT-BLOOMING EVENT

The exquisite, almost sacred flowers of the night-blooming cereus cactus open for only one night each year. This rare spectacular event absolutely calls for a special gathering. It can take years for a night-blooming cactus to flower, and when it does, its flowers stay open only until morning, expiring after sunrise.

People have been getting together to celebrate this floral event across cultures for centuries. In Honolulu, a half-mile-long hedge of night-blooming cereus covers a long stretch of stone wall, and on a much-anticipated summer night, thousands of creamy white blossoms open to the moonlight. Tourists and locals alike gather for this mystical and fragrant show.

It is said that much of the night-blooming cereus through-out the island of Oahu started as clippings that people have taken from this hedge.

Marie Antoinette commissioned the artist Pierre-Joseph Redouté to capture this fleeting beauty while she was impris-oned at the Temple (a medieval fortress in Paris). Witnessing the buds develop on the *Selenicereus grandiflorus* was said to have lifted the queen's spirits. He painted the opening flower at midnight before the royal family.

Get some friends together for a midnight drawing session. This spectacle calls for being present and ready to capture one of nature's rare moments. You can serve dragon fruit—the delicious, bright red fruit of the night-blooming cactus—and cactus-infused drinks like prickly pear margaritas. The flowers stay open until dawn, so this could turn into an all-night soiree.

Meditations and Rituals

Rituals and meditations can deepen your experience with and relationship to your moon garden. They are opportunities to connect with the feminine energy of the moon, to ground yourself quite literally in the earth, and to reflect on how the lunar phases may guide your own desires and growth. The prompts that follow invite you to grow with your garden in gentle ways.

CHARGE YOUR PLANTS

On certain days of the year, when the stars align in a particular configuration, Tibetan Buddhist monks meditate on their garden plants. The monks chant mantras over the plants to charge them with energy and healing powers. They then use the plants to make healing butter, oils, incense, salves, and jewel pills. (Jewel pills are medicinal pills made up of herbal remedies meant to treat many ailments and illnesses. Considered to be both medicine and blessings, blessed by the Buddha, they are wrapped in blue silk cloth. They are crushed before being taken during the new or full moon.)

Contemplate this practice in your garden. There are many ways you could channel your attention and affection toward your plants. You could sing to them or play them music.

You could mindfully water your plants and observe their leaves beginning to perk up afterward, nourished. As you enjoy the company of your plants, you could express gratitude to them for infusing you with their healing energy. Take a meditative moment to consider the reciprocal nature of this exchange.

PLANT AN INTENTION

The new moon is a time to set intentions—a time to seek clarity and contemplate what it is you want to cultivate, create, and manifest in your life. On the night of the new moon, plant a seed while setting an intention. You can devote a planter or a garden bed to this practice. As you contemplate your intention, hold the seed in your hand and feel its energy and potential. Transfer this intention onto and into the seed. Poke a shallow hole in the soil with your finger, place the seed in the hole while thinking about its germination, and cover it with the displaced earth. Gently pat down the soil. Water the seed and witness the soil absorbing it, quenched. Over the course of the following weeks, check in on your seed, continuing to water it with mindfulness and encouragement. As the seed germinates, witness its growth. Reflect upon the nurturing of your own intention, just as you watch the seed grow.

FEEL THE EARTH

Feel your garden's soil. Run your hands over the surface and press them into the earth. Pick up a handful of soil and sift it through your fingers as you focus on its texture. How does it feel? Does it slip through your fingers like sand or clump like a ball of clay? As you feel the earth in your hands, contemplate how soil is the medium from which all plant life grows. (P.S. Finding a worm is a good sign of healthy soil!)

AWAKEN YOUR SENSES

Stroll through or sit in your garden at night. Observe the colors of the sky, the dark moody blues blending with mauves and grays, each color gently fading into the next. Maybe you spent your day in front of a bright screen—let your eyes adjust to gradations of darkness and softer, gentler light. Look for the moon: What phase is it in? Absorb its light.

In the quiet of night, close your eyes, think of the plant life that surrounds you, and breathe deeply. Quiet your thoughts and release yourself from expectation and judgment. Be fully present with the plants. Touch their verdant leaves and feel their texture. Inhale the scent of their flowers and imagine this perfume filling your body. Something as simple as smelling the flowers can be a nightly ritual in your moon garden.

TRANSITION

Just like the moon, we have our own cycles throughout the days and months. We spend the workday making decisions, expending energy, and consuming external stimuli, and often we bring this home with us. Your moon garden can be a place to consciously shift or transition from day to evening, a shift that you can honor as a daily practice. Maybe this means keeping your phone far away, changing out of work clothes, or turning off all overhead lighting indoors. Exhale any restless energy you had earlier in the day; breathe in your arrival to a new phase of your evening. Journaling can allow you to process your day, transitioning you out of work mode. Your moon garden is a place to change rhythms, to shift from doing to being.

Writing with the Moon

Some people journal for self-discovery, uncovering things through the act of writing; others journal for catharsis, to release thoughts or emotions. Either way, journaling is like a psychic cleanse: As we jot down thoughts on paper, we release them from the mind. New ideas and inspirations can spring forth. Following are some prompts inspired by the lunar phases. As you sit in your garden, channel the moon's guiding light and turn to your journal as a place to release, explore, and reflect.

JOURNAL PROMPTS

 During the **NEW MOON** the moon is positioned between the sun and the earth. Thus, what we see is the "dark side" of the moon, the side not illuminated by the sun—meaning that we often cannot see it in the sky at all. The new moon is a time to look ahead and set intentions. What are your aspirations? Is there a journey that you are ready to embark on? What do you want to invite into your life?

 The **WAXING CRESCENT MOON** is the lunar phase just after the new moon, when the illuminated portion of the moon grows and looks like a crescent. During this phase, write about growth. In what areas of your life do you want to feel a sense of expansion or illumination? What would that journey look like?

 The **FULL MOON** occurs when the side of the moon facing the earth is fully illuminated by the sun. Use the full moon as an opportunity for reflection: Think back to an intention that you set at the new moon. Were you able to take steps toward this goal? In what ways do you already shine?

The **WANING GIBBOUS MOON** is the phase just after the full moon, when the moon appears to be shrinking but still looks two-thirds full. What do you want to shed from your life? What burdens you? Are there things that you could do without? What would it take to experience this release?

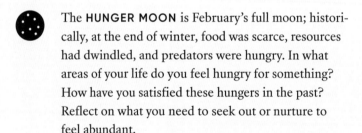

THE FOLLOWING FULL MOONS PRESENT OPPORTUNITIES FOR CONSIDERING BOTH SCARCITY & ABUNDANCE IN YOUR LIFE.

 The **HUNGER MOON** is February's full moon; historically, at the end of winter, food was scarce, resources had dwindled, and predators were hungry. In what areas of your life do you feel hungry for something? How have you satisfied these hungers in the past? Reflect on what you need to seek out or nurture to feel abundant.

The **SAP MOON**, also known as the worm moon, signals that spring has arrived. This full moon usually occurs in March, when birds migrate north to feast on emerging insects and when sap starts rising in maple trees, ready to be tapped for syrup. Just as the maple trees produce sap, what do you want to cultivate to add more sweetness into your life? Reflect on the people and things that bring you joy. What is dormant within you that you want to bring to the surface?

The **STRAWBERRY MOON** is June's full moon, named by the Algonquins in the northeastern United States and eastern Canada to reflect this region's strawberry harvesting season. In Europe it is called the Rose Moon because roses are in peak bloom in June. This is the last of the spring full moons and marks a cusp or transitional period. It is a time for goal setting, holding your head up high, and looking ahead, while also acknowledging gratitude for what you already have. Write down some ways that you feel proud of yourself. Savor this feeling of positivity and channel it toward the summer ahead of you. What do you envision for yourself moving forward?

The **HARVEST MOON** occurs in autumn. The moon is at its closest to earth, rising at its earliest and appearing brightest and fullest. Before electricity, this bright moonlight enabled farmers to extend their workday beyond sunset and harvest their crops late into the night during their busiest time of year. The harvest moon is a time to reap the fruits of your labor. What have you been working toward for which you are finally seeing progress or results? Recognize your achievements, however big or small, and give yourself credit.

Herbs and Teas for Winding Down

Having a nightly cup of tea in your moon garden can be a soothing ritual before bed. The calming properties of herbs like chamomile, lavender, and passionflower can help you wind down. If you have trouble falling asleep, an herbal tea with valerian root is an old remedy.

Brew a cup of tea, then find your favorite spot in the garden. While your tea steeps, be present. Contemplate all of the healing properties in the herbs, which grew from the earth, under the night sky. Slowly take a sip. Feel the warmth seep through your body. You may even be inspired to grow herbs to make tea from your own garden.

HERBS FOR DREAMING

Mugwort (*Artemisia vulgaris*) has been used for centuries for vivid dreaming, lucid dreaming, and exploring one's dream state. Its botanical name, *Artemisia*, comes from the Greek moon goddess Artemis. Considered a visionary herb, mugwort is said to allow one to see into their future. The leaves, stems, blossoms, and roots have all been used in folk medicine to treat anxiety, boost energy, regulate the menstrual cycle, relieve headaches and muscle aches, and more. If you're pregnant, avoid mugwort, as ingesting it may have unwanted side effects.

On nights that you want to embark on a lucid dream, make a cup of mugwort tea. Steep the dried leaves in boiling water for five to ten minutes. Strain the leaves and add a sweetener like honey or maple syrup—mugwort on its own has a slightly bitter taste. Or make a tea blend by adding passionflower and dried orange peel.

Artemisia grows prolifically in North America—you can harvest this plant yourself: Cut several stems, bundle them together with twine, and hang them upside down to dry. If you'd prefer other ways to use mugwort, bundle several stems together with twine and tuck them under your pillow or hang them near your bed. Keep your dream journal close by to record your dreams in the morning.

Beneath the Moonlight

Spending time outdoors in the thick of night offers a certain peace of mind, inflected by a sense of the expansiveness of the cosmos.

STARGAZE AND WATCH THE MOONRISE

Devote some time at night to identify spots in your garden that provide the best views of the sky, where the light is most dynamic at sunset, where you can stargaze and watch the moonrise. Set aside an evening around the full moon to watch the sunset and moonrise. You can look up the time when the moon rises and sets on any given day. Supermoons appear bigger and brighter than other full moons because they occur when the moon's orbit is at its closest distance to earth. Certain meteor showers visit annually, like the Perseids (near the prominent constellation Perseus), visible in North America. When the peak of the Perseids aligns with a new or old moon, it's worth staying up until dawn to watch. Keeping note, or even a calendar, of different celestial events can make your moon garden an intimate space dedicated to beholding the wonders of the universe.

MAKE A MOON ALTAR

Select a spot in your moon garden where the moonlight
consistently shines in most seasons. Add elements that are
significant to you and that celebrate the moon and its cycles,
such as shells and rocks you have collected on the beach
brought in from the lunar tides, or crystals like selenite and
moonstone, which are known for their yin (feminine) energy.
Some moonstone gleams with iridescence, and some selenite
crystals contain "flowers." Use candles with subtle scents
of jasmine or gardenia, or incense, like nag champa, a spicy
sandalwood scent reminiscent of the Moonlight Garden near
the Taj Mahal. Adorn your altar with cascading silver foliage
or a bud vase with white or pale-colored flowers. A cut white
magnolia or plumeria flower floating in a shallow bowl of
water, especially with floating candles, lends a mystical glow,
especially when meditating or setting intentions at your altar
in the evening.

WRITE A LOVE LETTER TO THE MOON AND BURY IT

The moon is a constant presence in our lives. Behind alpine
horizons, it rises; through mist and fog, it presides. On clear,
crisp nights, our moon joins a sea of stars to watch over us. You
are never truly alone with the moon in the sky and your garden
growing all around you. What would you say to the moon to
express your gratitude and devotion? Write a poem or a love
letter to the moon and bury it in the garden. What you write is
a secret you share only with Mother Nature. Your words will be
absorbed into the soil, and your letter will become a part of the
earth's memory.

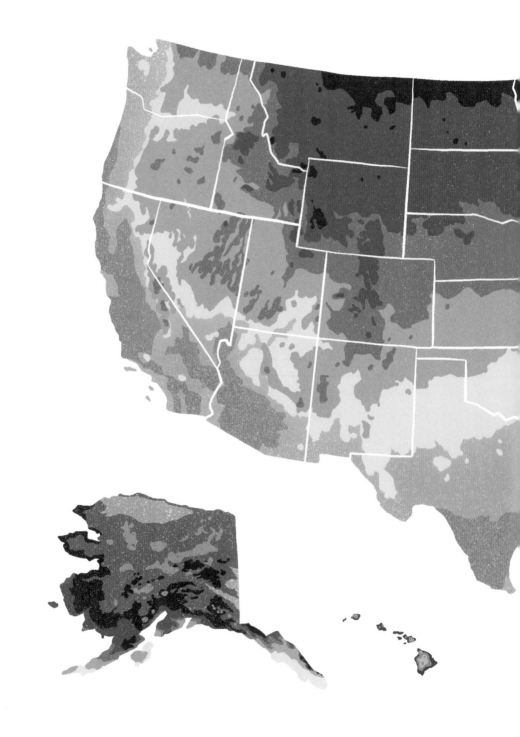

PLANT
HARDINESS
ZONE
MAP

AVERAGE ANNUAL LOW TEMPERATURE [°F]

1	*2*	*3*	*4*	*5*	*6*	*7*
-60 to -50°	-50 to -40°	-40 to -30°	-30 to -20°	-20 to -10°	-10 to 0°	0 to 10°

8	*9*	*10*	*11*	*12*	*13*
10 to 20°	20 to 30°	30 to 40°	40 to 50°	50 to 60°	60 to 70°

RESOURCES

Clifton, Joan. *Making a White Garden.* New York: Grove Press, 1990.

Kimmerer, Robin Wall. *Braiding Sweetgrass: Indigenous Wisdom, Scientific Knowledge, and the Teachings of Plants.* Minneapolis: Milkweed Editions, 2013.

Leendertz, Lia. *The Twilight Garden: Creating a Garden That Entrances by Day and Comes Alive at Night.* Chicago: Chicago Review Press, 2011.

Loewer, Peter. *The Evening Garden: Flowers and Fragrance from Dusk Till Dawn.* New York: Macmillan, 1993.

Moynihan, Elizabeth B., ed. *The Moonlight Garden: New Discoveries at the Taj Mahal.* Seattle: University of Washington Press, 2000.

Sackwell-West, Vita. *In Your Garden.* Marlborough: Oxenwood Press, 1996.

Storl, Wolf D. *Culture and Horticulture: The Classic Guide to Biodynamic and Organic Gardening.* Berkeley: North Atlantic Books, 1979.

Walliser, Jessica. *Attracting Beneficial Bugs to Your Garden: A Natural Approach to Pest Control.* Beverly, MA: Quarto Publishing Group, 2022.